Shahnaaz Ayub

Perfectly Easy Indian Food

An Essential Guide to Cooking Traditonal Indian Favorites

Published by Clink Street Publishing

Copyright © 2014 Shahnaaz Ayub

First edition.

ISBN: 978-909477-04-9
Ebook: 978-909477-05-6

Photographer: James Collier (Flickr:jamesvancollier)
Makeup artist and hairstylist: Rudina Belba
Also special thanks to Jacqueline Burke for her assistance

Dear Fal

I hope you enjoy cooking these recipes as much as I've enjoyed writing about them. Well done in the cooking course – you outdid yourself. Love

Shan xxx.

To my soul mate, Shahid, and my three
gorgeous children, Aleena, Zara and Zain.
Thanks for your love, patience, understanding
and, above all, believing in me more than I do myself.

Contents

Introduction

Indian food is loved by millions of people who have never visited the sub-continent but have been enticed by the smells and tastes of its wonderful cuisine. Being born and brought up in the United Kingdom, I have witnessed the evolution in British eclectic palates to the extent that today, Indian food is regarded as being the country's most popular cuisine. Think of all the succulent and aromatic dishes you have relished in your favourite Indian restaurant. Now think of the joy of serving up these ever popular recipes at your own dinner table.

The curry houses serve the "generic" curries that we have all come to love and I have tried to provide an interesting cross-section of recipes to include the well known favourites and others that may be less familiar but equally evocative and delicious.

The fear that most people have about cooking Indian food is borne from their thinking that it involves numerous spices and is time consuming. This is a myth. In reality, cooking Indian food uses a very basic technique and the proportion of spices should be added to suit your individual taste. A quick trip every so often to the Asian stores scattered in little Indias nationally, or even on-line from Indian spice companies, should be enough to equip you with your spices – many of which can be blended in one ingredient known as "garam masala", leaving the others to be stored away but ready to use when needed.

This book contains a glossary of spices, with explanations of their origin, so it makes it easier for you to tailor-make your dish to suit your taste buds. The dishes I have included in this book are easy and often quick to put together and are full of flavour.

We all have a preconception of food from different countries which, in the main, has been influenced by how the cuisine is presented in our own country. This is either mostly restaurant-led or a sauce in a jar in the supermarket. Once you have experienced the ease with which my dishes can be made, your days of curry from a jar will be over. This book is equally suitable for beginners and experienced Indian cooks. It is ideal for gourmet dinner parties, but handy for snacks, salads and barbecues too. Eating proper Indian food will be a revelation and you will often find that dishes are much lighter than expected, with a lot of importance placed on freshness, aroma and colour, as well as being balanced and nutritious.

Being a working mother of three young children I realise the importance of being able to cook dishes for their simplicity but equally they have to be full of flavour and pleasure. Sometimes, time is short and with this in mind I have included flavoursome dishes that can be cooked in minutes. Others are more indulgent dishes that take time but can add that real wow factor to your dinner party and really impress your guests. So whether you want an easy but tasty dish for a mid-week family supper or something special for when you are entertaining guests, you are sure to find exactly the right recipe here.

I have read and possess a library of books on Indian cuisine and I have only found a handful of dishes from each book appealing. In this book I have sought to include the "favourite" dishes I get asked about all the time, but I have also taken into account regional foods as, over time, people have acquired the taste for the more authentic food. I love Indian food and this book has been a real culinary journey for me, as I hope it will be for you.

Glossary

It's very easy to become completely daunted by the many spices used in Indian foods. Many of them can now be found in major supermarkets. I often watch very cautious shoppers in the Asian food aisles of supermarkets picking up packets of spices, examining them, smelling them, squeezing them and then nervously putting them back on the shelves and opting instead for the jarred version of the curry sauce they wanted to make. I feel my heart fall to my stomach each time and I have to resist the urge to give them reassurance in case they call Security. The truth is, it's really like anything in life – you won't know how simple something can be unless you have tried it first, and anything complicated can always be mastered after a few attempts. So don't lose heart if you get yourself into a pickle. It happens to the best of us. Just remember to persevere!

I am amazed by the selection of Indian spices I see in major supermarkets nowadays. What a sign of the times and proof of the fact that more people are experimenting and developing the eclectic palate with world cuisine. Generally the supermarkets will sell cumin, coriander, turmeric, cloves, cinnamon, cardamom, nutmeg, black pepper, fresh ginger and garlic, paprika and cayenne pepper. Other ingredients have to be searched out from Indian or Pakistani delicatessens, which can be found in all major cities and small towns as well. Yes, we're everywhere!

Try to buy the dry spices in their whole form, which you can grind when you need them. I tend to keep a two-month supply of ground garam masala stashed purely for its convenience, but don't leave it sitting around for any longer as it loses its taste and aroma. All the spices will stay fresh for longer periods if stored in a cool, dry, dark place in tightly lidded jars. You will feel a real sense of achievement when building up your spice wardrobe collection, and they will be ready to grind when you need them. Invest in a good electric coffee grinder for this task; they are compact and do the job beautifully. Just remember that you won't be grinding coffee in it again once it's had the experience of grinding the Indian pungent spices. Remember that the more freshly ground the spice is, the better its flavour will be. I can appreciate, however, the necessity to buy ground spices purely for the sake of convenience when you need to make those mid-week meals in minutes. Who has the time to get the electric coffee grinder out then? If you, like me, do buy some ground spices, remember to buy them in small quantities and store them as you would the whole-form spices. Lastly, always remember to label your jars. Even after twenty-five years of cooking I still find it hard to visually differentiate between ground cumin and ground coriander without tasting and smelling it first.

It's really important to know exactly which spices, seasoning and flavouring you are putting into your dish, and as you become more familiar with the individual tastes you will be able to create your own dishes to suit your personal taste. Here is a list of those that I have used in this book.

Asafoetida (Heeng)

This is a distinctive and pungent spice which is also known as devil's dung on account of its foul smell, which, you will be pleased to know, disappears on cooking. It adds a pleasant flavour to fish, meat and vegetables. It's great for digestion and is therefore added to pulses and dhals because of its anti-flatulence properties. It is best bought in its ground form. I have not included it in many dishes so get the smallest box available and make sure the lid sits tightly on the box when you store it. If you don't have any, leave it out. It won't make much difference to the taste.

Ata Flour
Also known as chapati flour, this is a blend of plain and wholemeal flour widely used for making bread. It is available from Asian food shops and many supermarkets. Well-sifted plain and wholemeal flour in equal quantities can be used instead.

Basmati Rice
This is white rice that is the most highly recommended in Indian cooking. It comes from the foothills of the Himalayas and is known as the Prince of Rices because of its fine flavour and aroma. Beware, however, as not all basmati rice is of the same quality and there are plans in India for greater control over which variety may be officially included in this group in order to protect its quality. Before cooking rice always make sure it's rinsed in several changes of hot water.

Bay Leaves
These are aromatic leaves from the bay laurel tree. They can be used in either the fresh or the dry form and can give a simple dish real depth.

Bengal Gram
Similar to a chickpea but smaller and with a dark brown skin, this is also known as chana dhal. Once skinned, the bean becomes a wonderful earthy yellow lentil.

Besan
This is also known as gram flour and is made from ground chickpeas. It is used to flavour and thicken curries and for making pakoras and bhajis.

Bicarbonate of Soda
This is also known as baking soda, which is used in the making of certain breads and pakoras to give fluffiness.

Black/Brown Cardamom Pods (Bardi Elaichi)
Whenever I look at these pods they always seem like they are past their sell-by date, but don't be fooled by appearances. They have a wonderfully strong flavour when cooked and are sometimes used in pilaus and biryanis.

Cardamom (Elaichi)
These are used in both sweet and savoury dishes. Cardamoms are one of India's favourite spices and are native to the country. The pods may be used whole or the seeds can be extracted and used alone. This will be made clear in each of the recipes that use this ingredient. Whole pods are usually removed and discarded before a dish is served or just left at the side of the plate whilst eating. Green cardamoms are the most common, but there are black and cream varieties. Generally the black ones (see above) are used in savoury dishes. The cream ones are the ones I refer to in my recipes unless specifically stated otherwise and are in all savoury dishes. The green ones are for the sweet dishes although you can use them in the savoury dishes if the cream ones are not available. The green cardamoms taste delicious when brewed in a cup of tea. Just put them in whole and discard before serving. Cardamom is great for digestion. It is also known for being the world's second most expensive spice.

Carom Seeds (Ajwain)
This is a small seed with a very strong flavour so you only ever need to use a little. If you taste a seed, you will be reminded immediately of an Indian restaurant, where you may well have tasted the seeds in the tandoori naan bread. It can also be used with fish. I recall a hot medicinal tip from my lovely grandmother, who taught me that half a teaspoon of carom seeds with a pinch of salt in a hot cup of tea is an instant cure for stomach pain.

Cayenne Pepper (Pisi Hui Lal Mirch)
This is made from dried red chillies and is referred to as the red chilli powder by Indian and Pakistani grocers. It also includes both the ground seeds as well as the dried flesh. It is always hard to know how hot people like their food so

always use a small amount for mildly hot food and a larger amount if you want it hotter. This is available in all supermarkets generally.

Chana Dhal (aka Bengal Gram)
This is a split yellow lentil with a slightly sweet taste. Chana dhal is used in a variety of vegetable dishes and as a binding agent.

Chapati Flour
A blend of wholemeal and plain flour that is used to make our most common flat breads. It's not available in supermarkets generally. If you can't get hold of it then substitute equal quantities of plain and wholemeal flour.

Chick Peas (Chana)
This is a round, nutty flavoured pulse which is widely used in many vegetarian dishes. It's available dried or canned and can also be ground to make the besan or gram flour used to make pakoras and for thickening sauces.

Chillies (fresh/hot/green and also known as Hari Mirch)
Be careful when handling cut green chillies and refrain from touching your eyes or mouth. Wash your hands as soon as possible otherwise you will "burn" your skin because the chillies contain an irritant. The fresh green chillies are about 5 to 10 centimetres long and green outside with white seeds inside. They are rich in vitamins A and C and give the dish a very special and fresh flavour. Removing the seeds before cooking tones down the heat of the dish. As a general rule, dark green chillies tend to be hotter than light green ones, which in turn tend to be hotter than red chillies. Small, pointed chillies are usually hotter than larger, more rounded varieties. Always store them wrapped up in newspaper unwashed in a plastic container in the refrigerator and discard any bad ones.

Chillies (whole/dried/hot/red and also known as Sabut Lal Mirch)
These are generally smaller in size than their green cousins and they are often thrown into hot oil for a few seconds until they puff up and their skin becomes dark. Take care in handling the same way you would with green chillies (see above).

Chilli Powder
This is made from dried ground chillies and is a hot spice to be used with caution. Beware as some brands are hotter than others.

Cinnamon (Dar Cheeni)
This is available in all major supermarkets in sticks or ground form. It's a warm and aromatic spice. If the recipe requires a ground form, then use this as it is difficult to grind the sticks. The sticks are not meant to be eaten. They are just used for their flavour and aroma.

Cloves (Long)
Available whole or ground, this warm spice is used in both savoury and sweet dishes. They are not meant to be eaten (although my mother sucks on cloves as a mouth freshener). You can get these in most supermarkets and they are a must in garam masala. They are also a natural cure for toothache due to the oil they contain. Simply bite down on the clove where it hurts and hold it there for a while.

Coconut
This comes in several different varieties and I admit that none of my recipes require it from the fresh fruit itself. Anyone who can successfully crack a coconut open and preserve all the milk inside without maiming themselves deserves an award in my book! I use the cream, desiccated and milk form in my recipes. The cream is available in cans and cartons and is made from coconut and water. The desiccated variety is dried, shredded coconut which is unsweetened and concentrated. The milk variety is pure unsweetened coconut milk and is available in cans. Certainly in the case of coconut cream you can also choose a lighter canned version if you so wish, which will contain less fat.

Coriander (fresh/green and also known as Hara Dhaniya)
This is undoubtedly my favourite herb and I use it not only for its flavour but frequently for garnish on savoury dishes. It

always makes the dish look amazing. This herb is very fragrant and is usually added at the end of cooking to preserve its fresh aroma. It's always sold in bunches, which must be washed thoroughly before use. Just the top leafy section is used, although I often use the stems as they contain as much flavour as the leaf although they are not as aesthetically pleasing. So be careful not to use the stem as garnish. If you possess green fingers then grow this in your back garden in a pot. To store fresh coriander, put the unwashed and uncut bunch into a container filled with water (like flowers in a vase) and just expose the leafy section. Cover the whole thing in a plastic bag and put in the refrigerator. It will last for weeks. This herb tastes amazing when chopped and mixed into scrambled eggs with salt and coarsely ground black pepper. My kids love it mixed in with chopped red onion in their tuna/mayonnaise sandwiches.

Coriander Seeds (whole or ground)
These round beige coloured seeds come from the flower of the coriander plant and are mild and aromatic in flavour. They are excellent for digestion when made into a warm tea. They have an unmistakable subtle flavour. When the seeds are powdered or ground, they are used as a base for many curries. If you buy them in their ground form, discard them after a couple of months as they will begin to taste a bit like sawdust. Good quality powder will be slightly green in appearance rather than brown. Alternatively you could buy the whole seeds and grind them yourself in small quantities in your electric coffee grinder.

Cumin (Zeera or Jeera)
This is a really important spice in Indian cooking and adds a lovely rounded flavour to the dish. This spice gives an earthy flavour when cooked in oil and a nutty one when dry roasted. It's great for digestion when made into a light warm tea. They are used in both their whole and ground forms and are available in all main supermarkets. The whole seeds keep their flavour a lot longer and may be ground very easily in an electric coffee grinder. The seed is rigid and greenish-beige in colour. This is not to be mistaken for black cumin (see below).

Black Cumin Seeds (Shah Zeera or Kala Zeera)
These are fine seeds and much darker in colour and more expensive than the regular cumin seeds. You will only find these in Indian and Pakistani shops. If you can't find them then use regular cumin seeds instead. The only recipes in this book that use black cumin are Hyderabadi Biryani and garam masala.

Curry Leaves (Kari Patta)
These are beautifully fragrant and add a taste of the south to any dish they are added to. The leaves are thought to smell and taste like curry powder whilst the taste is spicy. It is also nutty, which is a quality brought out when the curry leaves are lightly fried in oil until just crisp. They are often added as a herb in their whole form. They are not to be mistaken for bay leaves, which have a very different flavour and are not an appropriate substitute. They can be stored in the freezer wrapped in foil for convenience.

Fennel Seeds
This sweet spice tastes a little like liquorice. Roasted fennel seeds are used to freshen breath after meals and are a good cure for indigestion.

Fenugreek Seeds and Leaves (Methi)
This is a fresh herb used in a number of vegetarian dishes and in some meat dishes. Always discard the stalk as it's unpleasantly bitter and use only the small leaves. When using the seeds, add sparingly as they have a strong flavour. The aroma will remind you of curry houses. The leaves can only be found in Asian ethnic stores but I recently managed to get hold of frozen blocks in a supermarket, which is just as good and practical too.

Garam Masala
This literally translates as "hot spices" as it is an aromatic mixture of various spices. The mixture is used sparingly and generally added towards the end of the cooking. It's not a standard spice mixture and there are many different variations. I've come across numerous family recipes but the one here happens to be my favourite. If you can help it, please don't resort to the ready-made form (except in a dire emergency) – it's quite pallid as it tends to contain cheaper spices such as cumin and coriander, which are often substituted for the more expensive spices such as cardamom and cloves. Always grind it in small quantities so it stays fresh. This recipe makes about 3 tablespoons, which should last you a while.

1 tablespoon of cardamom seeds
5 cm stick of cinnamon
1 teaspoon of black cumin seeds (or use regular cumin seeds as a substitute)
1 teaspoon of whole cloves
1 teaspoon of black peppercorns
14 of an average sized nutmeg

Put all the ingredients in a hot non-stick pan on a medium heat for a couple of minutes. Make sure you don't burn the contents of your pan otherwise the taste will completely change. Then transfer the contents into your electric coffee grinder and grind until the mixture is finely ground. The aroma as you lift the lid will take your breath away. You must store this mixture in an airtight container in a dark, cool place.

Garlic (Laison)

This is indispensable in most Indian dishes and is best used in its fresh form, although I also keep a handy pre-prepared paste in a tight container in the fridge. One large clove is usually equivalent to half a teaspoon. Place the garlic cloves, say 115 grams, and 125 ml of water into a blender to make the paste and then store. It keeps for up to a month.

Ghee

This is clarified butter, i.e. butter that has had its milk solids removed. The process involves melting the butter over a low heat, then simmering it until all the moisture has evaporated and the milk solids have separated from the fat. The milk solids are then removed to leave the pure fat, which is excellent for frying at high temperatures. It has a long shelf life and can be found on supermarket shelves sold in tins rather than in the dairy section. I suggest using it in many of my recipes and the readymade versions are very good. It's usually a popular choice as it contains less saturated fat and is really delicious.

Ginger (Adrack)

This is a light brown knobbly looking aromatic fresh root and another essential in Indian cooking. It should be peeled before chopping or pulping. Never use ground ginger as a substitute but you can always have a stash of ginger paste for convenience. Use 115 grams of fresh root ginger, peeled and roughly chopped, and 125 ml of water and blend to a paste. Keep it in an airtight container in the fridge, where it will store for about a month.

Gingelly Oil

This is the same as sesame oil or "til" oil, which is derived from sesame seeds and readily available in all supermarkets. It has significant health benefits such as lowering cholesterol, is a source of anti-oxidants and it promotes healthy skin.

Gram Flour (see Besan)

Green Cardamom Pod (Chotti Elaichi)

This is usually used in sweet and savoury dishes and is admittedly one of my favourite spices. You can grind the seeds to make green cardamom powder. This is delicious when brewed in strong tea, but be sure to remove the pods before drinking.

Jaggery (raw sugar) and Palm Sugar

This is an unrefined form of sugar. It's dark, sticky and crumbly. It's made from the juice of crushed sugar cane so it's less sweet than ordinary white or brown sugar and has an extraordinary musky flavour. Palm sugar has a comparable rich, complex taste and is a reasonable substitute for Indian jaggery in cooking. Brown and demerara sugar lack this earthy quality but will still work if you can't get hold of jaggery. I have only ever found jaggery in Asian stores.

Kalonji (Nigella Seeds)

These tiny teardrop shaped black seeds have a slightly peppery flavour but without the bite and are used mainly in vegetable and fish dishes in Bengal. They are sometimes confused with onion seeds, which they resemble in appearance (see Onion Seeds for my comment on this). They have an earthy aroma. They are commonly used in pickling and I often sprinkle them on my naans before I bake them. I have only seen them sold in small packets in a few supermarkets, but they are available generally in Asian food shops.

Khoya

This is basically semi-solid thickened milk and I discovered the recipe by logic! It's much quicker than evaporating whole milk, which is laborious, to say the least. It basically involves thickening the milk to a point where all that is left are the milk solids. Here's how to make this eureka moment, super-easy khoya in your home:

3 cups of whole milk powder/full cream milk powder or full fat milk powder
300 ml of thickened/double/thick heavy cream
1 can (375 ml) of evaporated milk

Put all three ingredients into a microwave-safe bowl and whisk until smooth and creamy. Cook on high in the microwave for 6 minutes watching the dish carefully in case it boils over, whereupon you stop immediately and wait for 8 to 10 seconds. Start again and run until the 6 minute time is up. Take the dish out and stir well to break up the lumps, which are milk solids beginning to form due to the cooking. Put the dish back into the microwave and set again on high for 6 minutes. Watch for the first minute and then allow it to continue cooking. When the time is up, let the dish rest for 10 to 15 minutes. The khoya is now ready for use.

Mace (Javitri)

This is the lacy dried covering of the ripe nutmeg seed and has a similar, slightly bitter taste. It is sometimes available intact with nutmeg but is more usually sold in fragments, called blades, or ground. It has a wonderful flavour that goes very well with meat and chicken.

Mango Powder (Amchur)

This is used to flavour vegetarian dishes. It's a sour powder made from dried, raw, unripe mangos. It's great sprinkled over cooked tandoori foods because of its tangy flavour. It also acts as a great meat tenderiser.

Masala

This word simply means "spice", which could mean a single or a blend of spices. It could also be the base of a gravy that has been spiced.

Masoor Dhal (red lentils)

These red split lentils are widely available and used in many dishes. They are actually orange in colour and become much paler when cooked. They are so easy to digest and have a slight sweetness. They absorb their surrounding spices with ease.

Mint (Pudina)

This is a widely used herb often paired with lamb. Indian mint has a stronger flavour and more pungent aroma than the western varieties but, of course, feel free to use our western produce where required.

Moong Dhal (Mung Beans)

This split yellow lentil is quite similar to chana dhal, but smaller. It's one of the easiest to digest and has a subtle buttery flavour.

Mustard Oil

This is a yellow oil made from mustard seeds and is quite pungent when raw and then amazingly sweet when heated. It's often used in Bengal for cooking vegetables and fish and is a favourite oil throughout India for pickling. If you cannot get hold of it then use a ground nut oil but never, need I say, use the pharmaceutical variety for cooking!

Mustard Seeds (Rai)

All I can say is, once you have started using these seeds, you won't stop. They are perfectly round, tiny and dark reddish brown in colour. When you scatter them in hot oil, they effervesce spectacularly and turn the oil deliciously nutty. The larger, yellow variety, known as white mustard seeds, are much less pungent.

Onion Seeds

These are often confused with kalonji (Nigella seeds) and I often see in them in Indian cook books being referred to as one and the same. Most annoying, to say the least, when an author cannot undertake proper research! These small black seeds are used in many pickles and curries, especially with vegetables.

Panch Poran (Five Spice)
This is an Indian mix of five (panch) spices consisting of cumin seeds, onion seeds, mustard seeds, fenugreek seeds and aniseeds. If you want to make this five spice powder at home then take a teaspoon of each of the above and grind them. Store in an airtight container. You can find it ready made in all Indian supermarkets.

Paneer (Indian Cheese)
This is India's best known cheese and can be freshly made at home. Its firm texture means it can be cut into cubes, then fried or grilled whilst retaining its shape. If you want to make it at home then follow this simple recipe:

1 litre of milk
2 tablespoons of lemon juice

Bring the milk to the boil in a pan over a low heat, then reduce and simmer gently for a few minutes. Add the lemon juice and stir until the milk begins to curdle. Drain the mixture through a muslin cloth and then rinse the contents under cold water. Gather up the corners of the muslin cloth and tie them together. Squeeze gently to extract any moisture. Then form your paneer block into the required shape.

Pilau (aka Pilaf)
This is a term used for any spiced and seasoned rice dish. It can be a simple pilau or an indulgent one with a number of ingredients.

Pomegranate Seeds (Anardana)
These are added to vegetarian dishes to give them a tangy, acidic flavour. You can use fresh pomegranate seeds directly from the fruit or dried seeds, which are available in all Asian food shops.

Poppy Seeds (Khus Khus)
These are white poppy seeds that are quite different from the tiny black ones that are popular in the west. These skinless seeds have a smoother character and are often ground and used as a thickener.

Raita
A term used for yoghurt once it has ingredients added to it.

Red Lentils (see Masoor Dhal)

Rice Flour
Fine, white, powdery rice flour is commonly used for batters and dough in South India and to make soft rice noodle cakes. It can also be used as a thickening agent in the same way as cornflour. It has a mild flavour that's delicately sweet.

Rose Water (Kewra Water)
This is diluted rose-essence. It's a fragrant liquid extracted from rose petals and used in Indian puddings and drinks. It's available in some supermarkets and in all Asian food shops.

Saffron (Zaafran or Kesar)
This is the dried stamen of the crocus flower. It is very expensive but a little goes a long way and it keeps well in the fridge. It has a lovely musky flavour that works in both savoury and sweet dishes because of its delicious aroma and flavour, as well as a lovely yellow colour. It's available as threads (which I recommend you buy) or powder.

Salt (Namak)
Amounts of salt given in recipes can be adjusted to suit individual tastes but always err on the side of caution and add less to begin with as salt can always be added later but never taken away to give the true flavour of the dish. If you have

added too much salt then try adding yoghurt or cream to dilute the taste; but this addition depends upon the dish you are making.

Sesame Seeds (Til)
These are available almost everywhere in food shops nowadays. They have a wonderfully nutty flavour, especially after being roasted.

Split Black Gram (Urid Dhal)
This lentil is available with its hull, which is black and also known as Black Gram, or hulled, when it's creamy white. It takes quite a long time to cook and is used a lot in South Indian food for texture, as it is sautéed to a nutty crunch.

Stone Flour (Patthar Ka Phool)
This is a kind of lichen that grows on rocks and stones. When whole, it's used for other whole spices, tied in a muslin cloth and immersed in the liquid for slow infusion. When powered, it should be added at the end of cooking.

Tamarind (Imli)
Sour tasting and strongly flavoured, this is the sticky dried, dark brown pod of the tamarind plant. This tart fruit is commonly used in South Indian and Gujarati cooking and brings a tangy contrast to mild sauces. I grew up being very familiar with tamarind, being Hyderabadi. It's sold in blocks and has a long shelf life. The pulp is obtained by soaking a section of the block in hot water for 20 minutes to soften the fruit. Then push it through a sieve to remove any seeds and fibres. The resulting liquid is stirred into dishes. Tamarind paste is more convenient to use and is available in jars from Asian food shops. You can use lemon as a substitute.

Tarka
This is spiced oil where hot oil is spiced and flavoured and added to the cooked dish. The flavours are fresher and more vibrant than if you had added the spices during the cooking of the dish. The aroma is amazing, although I can recall childhood days when my mother would warn us in advance before doing her tarka. We would all take cover or leave the house for 5 minutes as the aroma permeated our clothes as much as it did the dish.

Toor Dhal
This split lentil is similar to chana dhal.

Toovar Dhal (split yellow pigeon pea lentil)
This orange split pea has a distinctive flavour and is available plain or in the oily variety. When cooked it completely breaks down into a smooth paste which you then spice up before serving.

Turmeric (Haldi)
This gorgeous yellow spice is one commonly used in nearly all of my savoury recipes. It makes the food yellow. Buy the ground powder but handle with care as it stains easily. It has amazing medicinal qualities as a digestive and antiseptic. It adds a mild, earthy flavour to the dish.

Vark
This is real silver tissue which is used for garnishing sweets as well as festive meat and rice dishes. Despite appearances, it is edible and must be handled very gently as it's very fragile. It's only found in some Asian stores.

Yoghurt (Dahi)
Yoghurt adds a creamy texture and a delicate tartness to many of our sauces. Be careful as yoghurt curdles when it's heated; always add a tablespoon at a time and wait until it has been absorbed before adding the next one. Any thick, creamy, plain yoghurt will work for the recipes in this book but avoid any brands that are very sharp and acidic in flavour.

Starters & Snacks

Indians are inveterate snackers and snacks play a hugely important part in every Indian household. I have to confess the starters are my favourite Indian dishes, which is why this section is more extensive than you would normally find in any Indian cook book. I still rush to get to an Indian function on time as I do not want to miss the starters, which are, in my opinion, the best part of the meal.

When I have a dinner party I tend not to serve a selection of veg and non-veg curries with rice and bread any more. I have now adapted the modern technique of serving an array of Indian tapas, which provides a wider choice with different flavours to tantalise the taste buds. It is an altogether more exciting way of presenting your food. Many of the dishes can be made in advance and are also perfect finger foods for any cocktail party.

Dhal and Spinach Soup

Serves 6-8

Serve this Indian-style soup with some warm grilled naan bread spread with lashings of garlic butter. This is an ideal recipe to make in advance and freeze.

2 teaspoons of cumin seeds
2 teaspoons of coriander seeds
1 tablespoon of ghee
2 medium onions, chopped
2 cloves of garlic, crushed
1 tablespoon of grated ginger
2 dried chillies, chopped
8 curry leaves, torn
2 teaspoons of black mustard
   seeds
1/2 teaspoon of fenugreek seeds
1 teaspoon of ground turmeric
Pinch of asafoetida
200 grams of masoor dhal (red
   lentils, rinsed and drained)
2 medium potatoes, chopped
1.25 litres of chicken stock
1 kilogram of spinach (preferably
   baby spinach), roughly chopped
2 tablespoons of tamarind pulp or 1
   tablespoon of tamarind paste
100 grams of coconut milk powder
   (or half a can of coconut milk
   if this is not available, and then
   halve the amount of boiling
   water you add)
250 ml of boiling water
Salt to taste

Cook the cumin and coriander seeds, stirring occasionally, in a dry frying pan until fragrant. Then blend until crushed to a fine powder.

Heat the ghee in a large heavy based pan and cook the onions, garlic, ginger, chillies, leaves, mustard seeds and fenugreek seeds, stirring occasionally, until the onions are browned lightly.

Add the crushed spices, turmeric and asafoetida and continue to cook, stirring occasionally, for 1 minute.

Add dhal, potatoes and stock to the pan, bring to the boil then simmer, covered, for about 15 minutes or until the potatoes are tender.

Stir in the spinach and cook for a further 2 minutes.

Using a hand blender, blend the soup mixture until pureed.

Add the tamarind, coconut milk powder and water and stir until the soup is thoroughly heated through.

Chicken and Yoghurt Soup

Home made soups are rarely thick in consistency in India. The emphasis is on flavours to rejuvenate the taste buds and induce your appetite. This light soup was always a popular starter in those traditional polo clubs we would often dine at during our stay in Hyderabad.

Serves 4–6

1 kilogram of raw chicken bones
6 tablespoons of vegetable oil
150 grams of red onions, peeled
  and finely chopped
250 grams of tomatoes, finely
  chopped
250 grams of yoghurt, preferably
  Greek yoghurt, whisked
3 green chillies (left whole)
2 tablespoons of crushed garlic
1 tablespoon of finely chopped
  ginger
1 tablespoon of chopped fresh mint
2 teaspoons of ground coriander
1 teaspoon of garam masala (refer
  to Glossary)
1/2 teaspoon of ground turmeric
1 teaspoon of red chilli powder
1 teaspoon of cumin seeds,
  roasted in a frying pan and then
  ground
2 teaspoons of finely chopped
  coriander
Julienne strips of tomato
Shredded cooked chicken, to garnish (optional)
Salt to taste

Baghar
2 teaspoons of vegetable oil1 teaspoon of cumin seeds
1/4 teaspoon of Nigella seeds
  (kalonji)
2 tablespoons of gram flour
1 teaspoon of cumin seeds

Bring about 1 litre of water to the boil in a large, heavy based pan. Add the chicken bones and blanch for 1 minute. Drain and set aside the bones.

Heat the oil in a pan. Add the onions and fry until golden brown. Add all the remaining ingredients, except the chicken bones and fresh coriander (and those for the baghar), and stir fry for 30 seconds. Add the chicken bones and fry for 5 minutes. Then add 4 litres of water and bring to the boil, skimming off the scum from the surface.

Reduce the heat to as low as possible and simmer gently for 45 minutes. The water will have reduced by this time.

Drain through a fine sieve into a clean pan and bring back to simmer.

Heat the oil for the baghar in a small frying pan. Add the cumin and onion seeds and fry until they start to crackle.

Add the gram flour and fry until it turns golden brown.

Add this mixture to the chicken stock and simmer for 10 minutes.

Before serving, garnish with the chopped fresh coriander, cooked chicken strips, if using, and julienne of tomatoes.

Pumpkin Soup

This is a South Indian recipe and totally transforms the western style of soup we have all come to know. This is perfect for a cold day. The recipe is so easy – even for absolute beginners. The soup is velvety smooth and so makes the perfect starter for the most sophisticated of dinner parties.

Serves 4

450 grams of pumpkin, weighed after peeling and removing the seeds, diced (or butternut squash if pumpkin is not in season)
3 tablespoons of oil
2 onions, chopped
2 bay leaves
1/2 tablespoon of chopped ginger
2 cloves of garlic
1 green chilli
1 tomato, skinned and chopped
1 tablespoon of chopped fresh coriander
750 ml of either vegetable or chicken stock
3 tablespoons of single cream
1 teaspoon of lemon juice
Salt to taste

Heat the oil and fry the onions and bay leaves until soft.

Puree the ginger, garlic and chilli in a small electric grinder and then add to the pan and fry for 1 minute.

Add the pumpkin and fry for 2 to 3 minutes.

Add the tomato, coriander and stock and then bring to the boil. Thereafter simmer for 30 minutes.

Remove the bay leaves. Puree in a blender and thin the mixture with a little more stock, if necessary.

Re-heat gently stirring in the cream, lemon juice and the salt to taste.

Samosas

Making samosas can be quick or time consuming depending on how much time you have on your hands. The quick method uses ready-made filo pastry sheets that are readily available in most supermarkets and Asian stores, whereas the other method incurs having to make the dough yourself. Needless to say, no pain no gain as the latter is much tastier. Read this section even if you are using the ready-made filo pastry sheets as it will tell you how to make the pastry cones into which the filling is placed.

Makes 28 samosas

Samosa Pastry:
225 grams of plain flour
2 teaspoons of salt
2 tablespoons of vegetable oil
80 ml of warm water

Chilli, Mint and Lamb Filling:
500 grams of lamb, minced
2 tablespoons of vegetable oil
1 medium onion, chopped
2 cloves of garlic, crushed
1 tablespoon of grated ginger
1/2 teaspoon of dried chilli flakes
2 teaspoons of ground coriander
2 teaspoons of garam masala
    (refer to Glossary)
1 teaspoon of ground turmeric
1 teaspoon of paprika (preferably
    sweet paprika)
2 tablespoons of lemon juice
2 tablespoons of finely chopped
    mint leaf
Salt to taste

Samosa Pastry:
Sift the flour and salt into a medium bowl. Make a well in the centre of the flour then add the 2 tablespoons of oil with just enough water to make a firm dough.

Knead the dough on a floured surface until smooth and elastic. Form into a ball. Cover with plastic wrap and stand at room temperature for 30 minutes.

Divide the dough into 14 equal pieces and roll each piece into a 14 x 20 cm oval. Then using a knife halve the oval widthways so you end up with 2 semi-circles. Repeat the process, keeping the remaining pieces covered with a damp cloth to prevent them from drying out.

Brush the straight edge of each semi-circle (not along the curve) with a little water. Roll into a cone shape.

Fill the cone with a heaped tablespoon of the filling and then press the top edges together to seal. If you are having difficulty with sealing the edges then make a paste using 2 tablespoons of flour and adding a little water at a time until it forms a gooey paste. Repeat with the remaining dough and filling. These samosas are now ready to deep fry.

If you are using filo pastry
This usually comes in square sheets which should be cut in half in order to make a rectangle. Using the same principle as above, make a cone, fill it and seal the edges.

Chilli, Mint and Lamb Filling:
Heat the oil in a large frying pan and cook the onion, stirring occasionally, until browned lightly.

Add the garlic, ginger, chilli and spices and cook, stirring occasionally, until you can smell the aroma of the spices.

Add the minced lamb mint and continue to cook, stirring occasionally, until well browned and fully cooked.

Remove from the heat and stir in the lemon juice and the mint.

Allow to cool fully before filling each of the pastry cones.

Deep fry the samosas in hot oil in batches until browned and crisp. Drain on absorbent paper.

Vegetable Samosas

Makes 28 samosas

100 grams of peas
100 grams of carrots, chopped
100 grams of potato, chopped
2 green chillies
2 cloves of garlic
1 tablespoon of chopped ginger
1/2 teaspoon of ground turmeric
1/4 teaspoon of ground coriander
1/2 teaspoon of ground cumin
1 tablespoon of oil
1 onion, sliced
1/2 teaspoon of salt
1 tablespoon of water
3 tablespoons of chopped fresh
   coriander
Juice of 1 lime
Oil for deep frying

Grind the spices to a paste, including the chillies, garlic, ginger, turmeric, coriander and cumin.

Heat the oil and fry the onion until browned.

Add the peas, carrots and potatoes and fry for 2 minutes.

Add the ground spices, salt and water. Cover and simmer until the vegetables are tender and the water is absorbed.

Add the coriander and lime juice. Allow to cool to room temperature.

Spoon the vegetable mixture into the cones and seal the edges carefully.

Deep fry in hot oil until browned.

Potato Cutlets (Aloo Tikki)

Serves 6–8

The word "aloo" means potato and "tikki" means a small cutlet or croquette. This is an all time favourite hit with kids and grown-ups alike; it is a popular street food in North India. I salivate thinking of a hot aloo tikki drenched in yoghurt, tamarind and hot chilli sauce!

65 grams of yellow split peas (otherwise known as toor dhal)
3 large potatoes, chopped
75 grams of gram flour
1 tablespoon of chopped mint leaves
1 tablespoon of chopped coriander leaves
2 teaspoons of garam masala
1 teaspoon of ground cumin
1 teaspoon of ground coriander
2 small fresh red chillies, finely chopped
1 egg yolk
1 tablespoon of lemon juice
2 teaspoons of salt
Extra gram flour for dusting
3 tablespoons of ghee
1 egg, lightly beaten

Put the dhal in a medium bowl and cover with water to soak for 45 minutes. Then drain.

Place the dhal in a medium pan and cover with cold water. Bring to the boil then immediately simmer, uncovered, for about 10 minutes or until just tender. Drain.

Boil, steam or microwave the potatoes until tender. Drain, then mash. Allow the potatoes to cool.

Combine the mashed potatoes, gram flour, herbs, spices, chillies, egg yolk, juice and salt in a large bowl. Stir in the dhal.

Mould the mixture into balls then flatten to form patties about 1 ½ cm thick. Dust the patties with the extra gram flour, shake off any excess.

Heat the ghee in a large non-stick frying pan and dip the patties, one at a time, in egg. Fry the patties until browned on both sides and then drain on absorbent paper.

Tip:
This is best served hot with a hot spicy sauce. An idea for a quick sauce with a real kick is:
6 tablespoons of tomato sauce with 2 tablespoons of tamarind pulp (or 1 tablespoon of tamarind paste) and 1 teaspoon of garam masala. Mix these together to form a dipping sauce. This is ideal for this dish.

Potato Cutlets with a Mincemeat Stuffing (Aloo Kheeme Ke Cutlets)

These are potato cutlets with a spicy lamb mint filling. You can make these in advance and keep them chilled for a few days covered in golden breadcrumbs. Then simply fry when required. This makes an ideal snack or even part of a meal. This goes really well with plain steamed basmati rice and a nice tarka dhal. Uhmm – the thought of this really takes me back to my childhood.

Serves 6

500 grams of potatoes
250 grams of lamb, minced
3 tablespoons of vinegar
3 tablespoons of lime juice
2 to 3 green chillies, finely chopped
8 to 10 mint leaves
1/2 teaspoon of chilli powder
1 medium sized onion, finely chopped
3 tablespoons of finely chopped coriander leaves
1 tablespoon of finely chopped garlic
1 tablespoon of finely chopped ginger
1 egg, beaten
100 grams of golden breadcrumbs
100 grams of gram flour
1/2 teaspoon of black pepper
Vegetable oil for deep frying
Salt to taste

Boil the potatoes until they are soft.

In a dry pan heat the gram flour until it turns brown.

Peel and mash the potatoes and add vinegar, salt, black pepper and the roasted gram powder. Mix thoroughly and keep aside.

In a pan, heat the oil and then fry the onion until lightly brown.

Add the ginger, garlic, chilli powder, salt, coriander leaves, chillies, mint leaves and mince. Cook until the water dries off.

Add the lime juice to the dry cooked mince.

Make 12 to 15 balls out of the mashed potatoes.

Apply a little oil to the palms of your hands and flatten the balls. Take a tablespoon of the cooked mince, place it in the centre of each flattened mash potato ball and cover it on all sides so that the mince is fully covered. Flatten it slightly.

Dip the patties into the beaten egg and cover with breadcrumbs, then shallow fry until golden brown on each side.

Seekh Kebabs (Minced Meat Kebabs)

This is minced meat with spices and grilled on skewers, ideally on a barbecue or else under the grill. This is a favourite mouth watering starter or good as finger food at a party. It can also be part of the main course. Everyone always asks me for the recipe for this one and I have to say that I used every charm I had in a desperate attempt to get all the ingredients from a very unassuming chef who works at a famous kebab house in my home town.

Serves 6

500 grams of lamb, minced
2 eggs
1/2 teaspoon of garam masala
(refer to Glossary)
1 onion, finely chopped
3 tablespoons of vegetable oil
3 tablespoons of finely chopped
coriander leaves
2 green chillies
1 tablespoon of coarsely chopped
ginger
2 cloves of garlic
2 tablespoons of melted ghee, for
basting
Salt to taste

Grind to a fine paste the coriander leaves, green chilli, ginger and garlic.

Add to the ground paste the garam masala, onion, salt, egg, mince and the oil.

Secure the minced meat mixture along the length of the skewers and either grill or barbecue until it becomes light brown, turning occasionally and basting with ghee.

Hare Masala Chicken

This literally translates into "green chicken", which quite understandably did not go down well with the kids when they first set eyes on it. I vividly recall the comment "Eeewww! Green chicken?" They did not dare say much more as they knew this was going to be their dinner. As it happens, they loved it. Its colour does not make it any less delicious and you are sure to be blown away by the aroma of the herbs. It's a cinch to make and very delectable.

Serves 4-6

1 kilogram of boneless chicken
   thighs, cut into bite sized pieces
3 tablespoons of melted ghee

For the marinade
1 teaspoon of coarsely chopped
   ginger
1 teaspoon of coarsely chopped
   garlic
2 green chillies, chopped
1/2 teaspoon of ground coriander
Pinch of cumin
Pinch of garam masala
100 grams of onions, roughly
   chopped
2 tablespoons of tamarind pulp (or
   1 tablespoon of tamarind paste)
200 grams of fresh coriander
   leaves
50 grams of fresh mint leaves
1/2 teaspoon of ground turmeric
2 tablespoons of coarsely
   chopped cashew nuts
3 tablespoons of water
Salt to taste

Put all the ingredients for the marinade into a blender and process to a smooth paste.

Marinate the chicken in the paste for at least 6 hours.

Place the chicken in an oven dish with the marinade and cook at 150 degrees C, gas mark 5, for 45 minutes, basting with the melted ghee occasionally. Continue to oven bake until cooked.

Fried Lamb and Potato Chops

Serves 4

This is crispy, delicious, healthy and shallow fried, which makes it more or less guilt free. My family love this and there is no sophisticated way to eat it; you have to use your hands.

500 grams of lamb chops
4 cloves of garlic, crushed
1 tablespoon of finely chopped
  ginger
1 onion, finely chopped
1 small green chilli, finely chopped
2 tablespoons of chopped fresh
  coriander leaves
1 tablespoon of ground coriander
  seeds
1 teaspoon of garam masala (refer
  to Glossary)
1 teaspoon of ground roasted
  cumin seed
1/4 teaspoon of ground red chilli
200 ml of water
Salt to taste

Coating
225 grams of mashed potato
1 tablespoon of chopped fresh
  coriander
1/2 teaspoon of garam masala
  (refer to Glossary)
1/4 teaspoon of ground red chilli
  powder
2 tablespoons of oil
1 egg, beaten
100 grams golden breadcrumbs

Place the chops, garlic, ginger, onion, chilli, coriander leaves, ground spices, salt and water in a heavy based pan and bring to the boil. Cover and simmer over a medium to low heat for 20 minutes.

Remove the lid and increase the heat to dry off any remaining water.

Push the meat and spices up the bones to leave about 2.5 cm of clean bone.

Mix together all the coating ingredients except the egg and press around the chops.

Heat the oil in a frying pan in order to shallow fry. Dip the chops in the beaten egg and then coat with the breadcrumbs and fry until golden brown on both sides.

Stuffed Meatballs (Nargis Kebab or Indian Scotch Eggs)

Makes 8

This is a wonderful appetizer and also never fails to impress as a side dish. This is our Indian "desi" version of Scotch Eggs and consists of a boiled egg covered in a shell of spicy mince meat. It sounds exotic and tastes it too. Despite looking deceptively complicated, it's a fairly easy dish to make.

550 grams of lamb, minced
1 onion, roughly chopped
1 garlic clove, roughly chopped
1 tablespoon of roughly chopped ginger
40 grams of gram flour
1 teaspoon of ground cumin
1 tablespoon of ground coriander
1/2 teaspoon of chilli powder
1 egg, lightly beaten
Salt and pepper to taste
8 hardboiled eggs, shelled
Ghee or vegetable oil for deep frying plus extra for greasing

Place the onion, garlic and ginger in a food processor and blend to a paste.

Place the lamb in a bowl and add the onion paste.

Add the flour, cumin, ground coriander, chilli powder and beaten egg and season to taste with salt and pepper. Mix with your hands until thoroughly blended.

Divide the mixture into 8 equal sized portions and form each portion into a ball by rolling in the palms of your hands. Flatten into patties and place a hardboiled egg in the centre of each. Shape the meat mixture to enclose the egg completely. Place the balls in a lightly greased dish, cover with cling film and leave to rest in the refrigerator for 30 minutes.

Heat the fat in a deep fat fryer or large, heavy based saucepan to 180 degrees C or until a cube of bread is browned in 30 seconds.

Cook the meatballs, in batches, for 2 to 3 minutes, or until golden brown. Remove with a slotted spoon and drain on kitchen paper.

Vegetable Pakoras

Classic Indian finger food that no one can resist. It's known for its sheer versatility. Basically you can use any root vegetables so feel free to experiment. This is perfect for a rainy day at home with a hot steaming cup of tea. It is also ideal for any cocktail party.

Whilst frying, make sure the oil is not too hot as the pakoras will not end up crispy and will possibly be raw on the inside. If the oil is not hot enough, the pakora will be greasy. They are always best served hot with a tamarind dip or standard tomato sauce. My son made a very unexpected discovery by making a hot vegetable pakora sandwich with white bread and tomato sauce. What a fabulously delicious invention that was and just proves that the apple doesn't fall too far from the tree.

Serves 4–6

Batter
250 grams of gram flour, sifted
1 tablespoon of oil
2 tablespoons of chopped fresh coriander
1 tablespoon of dried pomegranate seeds
1 teaspoon of garam masala (refer to Glossary)
1 teaspoon of ground red chilli powder
1 teaspoon of ground roasted cumin
1 small chilli, chopped
Salt to taste
Lukewarm water

Vegetables
1 aubergine, diced
1 carrot, diced
2 courgettes, diced
Oil for deep frying

Place the flour in a bowl and rub in the oil.

Mix in all the ingredients except the vegetables and gradually blend in the water to make a thick batter.

Dip the vegetables into the batter.

Heat the oil over a medium heat in a deep fat fryer or a large, heavy based saucepan to 180 degrees C or until a cube of bread browns in 30 seconds.

Place tablespoons of the mixture into the hot oil a few at a time and fry until golden brown on all sides, turning them over until cooked.

Onion and Spinach Pakoras

Pakoras are one of the most delicious, versatile and easy to make snacks. I often take a plate of them as my contribution to a drinks party instead of a bottle of wine. No surprise – it gets all the attention and I usually spend the rest of the party taking the credit and giving the recipe! It goes really well with a fruity chutney. Whilst making this dish remember that spinach and onions will release water once they are mixed with salt and spice powders, so go cautiously when adding the water.

Serves 4–6

Batter
250 grams of gram flour, sifted
1 tablespoon of oil
2 tablespoons of chopped fresh
   coriander
1 tablespoon of dried pomegranate
   seeds
1 teaspoon of garam masala (refer
   to Glossary)
1 teaspoon of ground red chilli
   powder
1 teaspoon of ground roasted
   cumin
1 small chilli, chopped
Salt to taste
Lukewarm water

Vegetables
1 medium onion, thinly sliced
50 grams of spinach (preferably
   baby spinach), chopped
Vegetable oil for deep frying

Place the flour in a bowl and rub in the oil.

Mix in all the ingredients except the onion and spinach and gradually blend in the water to make a thick batter.

Stir the onion and spinach into the batter.

Heat the oil over a medium heat in a heavy based saucepan to 180 degrees C or until a cube of bread browns in 30 seconds.

Place tablespoons of the mixture into the hot oil, 7 or 8 at a time depending on the size of your pan, and fry until golden brown on all sides, turning them over until cooked.

Prawn Pakoras

Serves 4–6

A wonderfully tasty appetiser and definitely my favourite variety of pakora. This is traditionally a South Indian prawn recipe. It is an easy, quick and delicious method.

450 grams of peeled prawns
    (cocktail sized)
50 grams of gram flour
2 tablespoons of water, approxi-
    mately
2 onions, sliced
5 green chillies, chopped
1 teaspoon of pomegranate seeds
Pinch of bicarbonate of soda
    (baking soda)
Salt to taste
Vegetable oil for deep frying

Place the flour in a bowl and add just enough water to make a thick batter.

Stir in the remaining ingredients.

Heat the oil in a deep fat fryer or large heavy based saucepan to 180 degrees C or until a cube of bread browns in 30 seconds.

Drop a tablespoonful of the batter at a time into the oil and fry until golden brown.

Tandoori Fish

Serves 4–6

This makes a great starter for fish lovers. Be sure to serve it with a hot sauce and a lemon wedge. This works equally well with catfish or tilapia. As with all Indian recipes, feel free to adjust the spices to your requirements. The tandoori spices gives it a tangy, mildly spiced taste which does not interfere with the delicate flavours of the fish.

900 grams of cod, cut into pieces
  or left whole
Salt to taste
4 tablespoons of lemon juice
4 tablespoons of wine vinegar
6 large cloves of garlic
1 tablespoon of coarsely chopped
  ginger
1 onion, coarsely chopped
2 teaspoons of garam masala
  (refer to Glossary)
1 teaspoon of ground cumin
1 teaspoon of ground turmeric
1/2 teaspoon of ground mace
1/2 teaspoon of grated nutmeg
1/2 teaspoon of ground red chilli
2 tablespoons of oil
4 tablespoons of ghee, melted

Blend the lemon juice, wine vinegar, garlic, ginger and onion to a smooth paste in a food processor. Add the ground spices and a pinch of salt. This is your marinade.

Add the marinade to the fish by rubbing it into the fish. Ensure the fish is covered with the marinade. Cover and leave to marinate for 2 hours, turning occasionally.

Heat the oil in a non-stick pan. Lift the fish from the marinade (being sure to reserve the marinade) and fry lightly on all sides for about 5 minutes.

Place the fish in a large, non-metallic ovenproof dish.

Pour the marinade into a pan and cook in half of the melted ghee until the mixture has been reduced and it is light brown.

Rub this mixture over the fish. Then pour over the fish the other half of the melted ghee.

Bake the fish in a pre-heated oven at 200 degrees C, gas mark 6, for about 10 minutes. Carefully turn over the fish and baste it with the marinade. Bake for a further 15 minutes.

This dish can be served hot or cold, either as part of a main course or as a starter snack.

Lucknow-style Shami Kebabs

I don't know anyone who doesn't like shami kebabs. They are basically made up of finely minced lamb mixed with spices and chana dhal then held together with egg and fried in flat patty shapes. The Hyderabadi version is shikampur, which I cannot reveal – at least not in this book as the recipe is a cautiously guarded family secret that my parents' generation take extremely seriously; I am loyally bound by all relatives privy to this recipe to reveal neither the ingredients nor the method. So in this recipe I have gone for the next best thing. These kebabs are welcomed whether at lunch time in a pitta with fresh salad and chunky tomato slices, or at dinner with steamed rice and a nice dhal. They also make a fabulous picnic snack. You can make batches of these in advance and freeze them in their cooked form – such a life saver for us busy mums.

Serves 4–6

900 grams of minced lamb
2 onions. chopped
100 grams of yellow split peas
10 black peppercorns
2.5 cm cinnamon stick
6 black cardamom pods
8 cloves
4 bay leaves
1 tablespoon chopped ginger
10 cloves of garlic. chopped
3 dried red chillies
3 cups of water
1 teaspoon garam masala (refer to Glossary)
Salt to taste
Oil for frying
1 egg. beaten

Mix all the ingredients, except the oil and the egg, in a large, heavy based pan and simmer for about 25 minutes until the meat is tender, stirring occasionally.

Drain, discard the liquid and leave to cool. Remove and discard the cardamom skins.

Blend the mixture then shape into flat patties.

Dip in the beaten egg and then fry in a lightly greased pan for about 15 minutes on each side until brown.

Deep Fried Lamb in Batter

Cubes of lamb are first cooked in a mixture of garlic, ginger and spiced yoghurt and then coated in batter and deep fried to make a satisfying and substantial meal. This is also delicious made with diced chicken instead of lamb. Make sure the lamb cubes are cold before coating them with batter otherwise they will not be crisp when they are cooked. This makes a great party snack. If served as a main meal then accompany it with plain steamed basmati rice and a vegetarian dish that has plenty of sauce.

Serves 4

675 grams of diced lamb
4 tablespoons of natural yoghurt
2 teaspoons of chilli powder
1 teaspoon of ground turmeric
Salt to taste
2 tablespoons of ghee or vegetable oil plus vegetable oil for deep frying
3 cloves of garlic, finely chopped
1 1/2 tablespoons of finely chopped ginger

Batter
225 grams of gram flour
1/2 teaspoon chilli powder
1 teaspoon of salt
5 tablespoons of natural yoghurt
225 ml of water

Mix the yoghurt, chilli powder, turmeric and a pinch of salt together in a bowl and reserve.

Heat the ghee in a karai or large frying pan. Add the garlic and ginger and cook, stirring frequently, for 2 minutes. Add the lamb and cook, stirring frequently, until browned all over. Stir in the yoghurt mixture and simmer gently, stirring occasionally, for 30 minutes or until the lamb is tender, then leave to cool.

To make the batter, sift the flour, chilli powder and salt into a bowl. Stir in the yoghurt, then gradually beat in the water to make a smooth batter. Leave to rest for 30 minutes.

Heat the vegetable oil in a deep fat fryer or heavy based saucepan until a cube of bread browns in 30 seconds. Dip the lamb in the batter, then deep fry. This must be done in batches for 3 to 4 minutes each time, or until golden brown. Drain each batch on kitchen paper and keep warm while you cook the remainder.

Meat Dishes

From kebabs to curries, the choice is huge. I have included richly flavoured stews, quick stir fries, succulent roasts, together with colourful tandoori dishes for baking or barbecuing. Lamb is undoubtedly India's favourite meat and it is usually cooked with the bones in to add extra flavour. I always purchase lamb (spring lamb if I am lucky) rather than mutton, which is generally tougher and tends to become "rubbery". People may purchase mutton and cook the dish in a pressure cooker. Try to avoid this. It is always worth getting good quality meat from trusted butchers. I usually ask the butcher for a mixture of hind leg and shoulder cuts with the bone in and then cut into bite sized pieces. It is always best to cook the dish a few hours before serving to help mature the spices, then re-heat before serving. This means these dishes (apart from biryanis included in the rice section) can be cooked in advance.

Rogan Josh

Serves 6

This is a popular restaurant classic that's really easy to make at home. What's great about this dish is that you don't have to use lamb. It works just as well with chicken, prawns or root vegetables which will all require less cooking time than lamb. This dish has a Persian origin and is one of the signature recipes of Kashmiri cuisine. Rogan is Persian for "oil" whilst Josh means "passion". When you cook such a delicacy, you only pray for more.

1 kilogram of diced lamb, with or without the bone
225 ml of natural yoghurt
1/2 teaspoon of cayenne pepper
1/4 teaspoon of asafoetida
1 tablespoon or coriander seeds
1 tablespoon of cardamom seeds
1 teaspoon of cumin seeds
1 teaspoon of white poppy seeds
8 black peppercorns
4 cloves
1 1/2 tablespoons of chopped fresh root ginger
4 garlic cloves
2 tablespoons of almonds
300 ml of water
4 tablespoons of ghee or vegetable oil
1 onion, chopped
1 teaspoon ground turmeric
2 tablespoons of chopped fresh coriander
1 teaspoon garam masala (refer to Glossary)
Salt to taste

Mix the yoghurt, cayenne and asafoetida together in a large, shallow dish. Add the lamb and toss well to coat. Cover and set aside.

Place the coriander, cardamom, cumin and poppy seeds in a food processor with the peppercorns, cloves, ginger, garlic, almonds and 4 tablespoons of the water to make a paste, adding a little more water if necessary.

Heat the ghee in a heavy based deep pan. Add the onion and cook over a low heat for 10 minutes or until golden. Stir in the spice paste and turmeric and cook, stirring occasionally, for 5 minutes. Add the lamb, with its marinade, and increase the heat to high and cook, stirring continuously, for 10 minutes. Reduce the heat, and cover for 45 minutes.

Stir in the remaining water and simmer until the meat is tender. Stir the chopped coriander and garam masala into the lamb and season with salt to taste. Cover and then cook for a further 25 minutes.

For an aromatic garnish, heat 1 tablespoon of oil and add 1 tablespoon of cumin seeds and 2 bay leaves. Cook for 2 minutes and then sprinkle the entire contents over the curry.

Boti Kebabs

Serves 4

This is a classic tandoori dish, but works well cooked under a conventional grill. It is important to use a glass or ceramic dish whilst the meat is marinating as the vinegar can react with metal and will taint the flavour of the meat. A popular South Indian dish, these kebabs are tender, fragrant and filled with flavour.

450 grams of lamb, diced
1 teaspoon garlic paste (see Glossary)
1 teaspoon ginger paste (see Glossary)
1 teaspoon chilli powder
1 tablespoon ground coriander
1 tablespoon of red wine vinegar
2 tablespoons lemon juice
Salt to taste
1 green pepper, de-seeded and cut into chunks
1 large onion, cut into wedges
4 tomatoes, quartered
Vegetable oil for brushing
Fresh coriander sprigs and lime wedges for garnish

Mix the garlic paste, ginger paste, chilli powder, ground coriander and vinegar in a large, shallow, non-metallic dish. Add the lamb and stir to coat. Cover with clingfilm and leave to marinate in a refrigerator for 4 to 6 hours, stirring occasionally. It is important to use a glass or ceramic dish while the meat is marinating, as vinegar can react with metal and will taint the flavour of the meat.

Heat the grill to medium. Sprinkle the lemon juice over the meat, then thread the meat onto the skewers, alternating with the chunks of green pepper, onion wedges and tomato quarters.

Brush with vegetable oil and grill, turning frequently and brushing with more oil if necessary, for 5 to 6 minutes, or until the lamb is browned all over and cooked through.

Garnish with coriander sprigs and lime wedges before serving.

Tip:
This is delicious wrapped in fresh naan bread filled with salad and mint yoghurt.

Balti Lamb/Beef Curry

Balti dishes are quick stir fried curries. They were introduced to the west by Pakistan's Multani community, but are also widely cooked in Kashmir and other northern regions of India. I always add that "wow" factor when I serve this dish at parties by bringing it to the table in those mini karahis you can purchase in department stores or cash and carry Asian stores. This is quite a dry dish that goes hand in hand with fresh naan bread and a yoghurt raita on the side. The lamb can be substituted for chicken or prawns, both of which will require less cooking time.

Serves 4

450 grams boneless cubed lamb
    or rump steak, cut into thin strips
2 tablespoons ghee or vegetable
    oil1 onion, thinly sliced
1 clove of garlic, finely chopped
1 1/2 tablespoons grated ginger
2 fresh red chillies, de-seeded and
    finely chopped
1 green pepper, de-seeded and
    finely sliced
1 yellow pepper, de-seeded and
    finely sliced
1 teaspoon of ground cumin
1 tablespoon garam masala (refer
    to Glossary)
4 tomatoes, chopped
2 tablespoons lemon juice
1 tablespoon water
Salt to taste
Chopped coriander to garnish

Heat half the ghee in a pre-heated wok or large, heavy based frying pan. Add the onion and cook over a low heat, stirring occasionally for about 8 to 10 minutes, or until golden. Increase the heat to medium, add the garlic, ginger, chillies and meat and cook, stirring occasionally, for 5 minutes, or until the meat is browned all over. Remove with a slotted spoon. Reserve and keep warm.

Add the remaining ghee to the wok, and then add the peppers and cook over a medium heat, stirring occasionally, for about 4 minutes or until softened. Stir in the cumin and garam masala and cook, stirring, for 1 minute.

Add the tomatoes, lemon juice and water, season with salt to taste and simmer, stirring occasionally, for 3 minutes.

Return the meat mixture to the wok and heat through.

Garnish with chopped fresh coriander before serving. The lamb can be substituted with chicken or prawns, both of which will require less cooking time.

Classic Lamb or Beef Korma (otherwise known as "Shahi Korma")

This is a royal lamb dish with an almond garnish and a creamy sauce. It owes its ancestry to Persian food. Cloves have a distinct aroma and flavour so use them sparingly as they may overpower the finished dish. This is a great curry and has become a real favourite in our household. The lamb can be easily substituted for chicken or prawns, both of which will require less cooking time.

Serves 6

1 kilogram lean beef or lamb (cubed). If using lamb then keep the bone in for extra flavour.
300 ml vegetable oil
3 onions, finely chopped
1 1/2 teaspoons garam masala (refer to Glossary)
1 1/2 teaspoons ground coriander
1 1/2 teaspoons finely chopped ginger
1 1/2 teaspoons crushed fresh garlic
1 teaspoon salt
150 ml of natural yoghurt
2 whole cloves
3 green cardamom pods
4 black peppercorns
600 ml of water

To garnish
6 soaked, peeled and chopped almonds
2 sliced fresh green chillies
A few coriander leaves

Heat the vegetable oil in a large, heavy based frying pan. Add the onions and stir fry for 8 to 10 minutes until golden. Remove half of the onions and reserve.

Add the meat to the onions remaining in the frying pan and stir fry for 5 minutes. Remove the frying pan from the heat.

Mix the garam masala, ground coriander, ginger, garlic, salt and yoghurt together in a large bowl. Gradually add the meat to the yoghurt and spice mixture and coat the meat on all sides. Place the meat mixture in the frying pan, return to the heat, and stir fry for 5 to 7 minutes or, until the mixture is nearly brown.

Add the cloves, green cardamoms and black peppercorns. Add the water, reduce the heat, cover and simmer for 45 minutes to an hour. If the water has completely evaporated, but the meat is still not tender enough, add another 300 ml of water and cook for a further 10 to 15 minutes, stirring occasionally.

Just before serving garnish with the reserved onions, chopped almonds, green chillies and fresh coriander leaves. The lamb can be substituted with chicken or prawns, both of which will require less cooking time.

Nargisi Kofta

Serves 4–6

Kofta is an Indian meatball. This is a wonderful dish to present if you want to impress your guests and family members and is incredibly simple to make. It is an Indian version of scotch eggs in a curry. In other words, minced meat stuffed with boiled eggs. Add it to a dinner party menu and friends will think you have been slaving away all day. This dish sounds exotic and tastes it too.

500 grams of minced lamb
2 tablespoons ground poppy
    seeds
1 tablespoon chopped fresh corian-
    der
1 tablespoon natural yoghurt
1 teaspoon garam masala (refer to
    Glossary)
3 large cloves of garlic. crushed
1 tablespoon of coarsely chopped
    ginger
1 onion. coarsely chopped
1 egg. beaten
Salt to taste
Oil for deep frying
4 - 6 hard boiled eggs

Sauce
5 tablespoons of ghee or oil
4 cloves
4 black peppercorns
2 bay leaves
2.5 cm cinnamon stick
1 black cardamom pod
2 onions. finely chopped
3 large cloves of garlic
1 tablespoon of coarsely chopped
    ginger
3 tablespoons of water
2 teaspoons of ground coriander
1 teaspoon of ground roasted
    cumin
1/2 teaspoon of ground red chilli
1/2 teaspoon of turmeric
Salt to taste
400 grams of canned tomatoes.
    chopped
150 ml of natural yoghurt
500 ml of water

Garnish
12 teaspoon garam masala
Fresh coriander. chopped
1 small green chilli. chopped

Blend all the main ingredients to a smooth paste in a food processor.

Divide into 10 equal portions. Using oiled hands shape the meat into balls, then flatten each ball and place a hard boiled egg in its centre and then shape the meat to enclose the egg completely forming a ball.

Heat the oil and fry the koftas, in batches if necessary, until golden brown on all sides. Remove and set aside.

To make the sauce, heat the ghee or oil in a heavy based pan and fry the whole spices and 1 onion until golden brown.

Blend the remaining onion, the garlic, ginger and water to a smooth paste in a food processor then stir it into the pan and cook until golden brown.

Stir in the ground spices, salt and tomatoes and cook until all the liquid has been absorbed and the oil appears on the surface.

Stir in the yoghurt and cook until all the liquid has been absorbed. Add the water and bring to the boil.

Add the fried kofta to the sauce and simmer for 10 minutes, uncovered. Just before serving sprinkle the garam masala over the top together with the chopped green chilli and the coriander.

Lamb Kheema

This is a mouth watering spicy lamb mince curry. Every bite is full of taste. Mince is an all-time useful standby as it is quick to cook and adaptable. This kheema is a fast and spicy way of preparing a quick mid-week meal which is easy to make with store cupboard spices and which requires nothing more than a naan bread as an accompaniment.

Serves 4

450 grams of fresh lamb mince
2 tablespoons of ghee or vegetable oil
1 onion, chopped
1 cinnamon stick
4 cardamom pods, lightly crushed
1 curry leaf
4 cloves
1 teaspoon ginger paste (refer to Glossary)
1 teaspoon garlic paste (refer to Glossary)
2 teaspoons ground coriander
2 teaspoons ground cumin
1 teaspoon chilli powder
150 ml natural yoghurt
1 tablespoon dried fenugreek leaves
Salt to taste
Fresh coriander, chopped, to garnish

Heat the ghee in a karai, wok or large, heavy based saucepan. Add the onion and cook over a low heat, stirring occasionally, for about 5 minutes or until softened.

Add the cinnamon stick, cardamoms, curry leaf and cloves and cook, stirring constantly, for 1 minute, then add ginger paste and garlic paste and cook, stirring constantly, for a further 1 minute.

Add the lamb mince and sprinkle over the ground coriander, cumin and chilli powder. Cook for 5 minutes, or until the lamb is lightly browned, stirring and breaking up the meat with a wooden spoon.

Stir in the yoghurt and fenugreek and season with salt to taste. Cover and cook over a low heat for 20 to 30 minutes, or until the lamb is tender and the liquid has been absorbed. Discard the curry leaf, the cinnamon stick and, if possible, the cloves.

Garnish with coriander before serving.

Lamb Dopiaza

Serves 4

Dopiaza translates to "two onions". This is a wonderful traditional dish with lamb cooked to tenderness with onions and quite mild spices. It is quite a simple curry recipe to make at home and very rewarding, with all the succulence and flavour you would expect if you were eating out in a good Indian restaurant.

450 grams lamb (with or without the bone)
3 tablespoons oil
1/2 teaspoon ground cumin
1 to 2 green chillies, de-seeded and chopped
1 teaspoon of sugar
5 onions, sliced
2 tablespoons of fresh, grated ginger
6 cloves of garlic, crushed
Salt and pepper to taste
2 tablespoons of white wine vinegar
250 ml water

Heat the oil in a heavy based pan and fry the cumin and chillies for a few seconds.

Add the sugar and fry for a few seconds.

Add 3 onions and fry until golden.

Stir in the ginger and garlic and fry until brown.

Add the lamb and fry until browned on all sides.

Add the salt and pepper, white wine vinegar and water and stir well and bring to the boil.

Cover and simmer for about 40 minutes until the lamb is tender. Add the remaining onions and then cover and simmer for a further 20 minutes.

Oven Baked Minced Lamb (Dum Ka Kheema)

This dish was a culinary tradition in the Nizam's household and, therefore, a dish very close to my heart. My dear aunt, now sadly widowed, was married to the grandson of the last Nizam of Hyderabad. Hence, I was immediately drawn to perfecting this dish that we grew up enjoying at many of our lavish dinner parties. This is spicy and aromatic and makes a perfect marriage with fresh naan bread or plain paratha. I suppose you could compare this to the American dish meatloaf. It basically consists of mince marinated in spices and yoghurt and then compressed in an oven dish and baked. The spices make the lamb flavoursome. I love this recipe as it's so fiery and always satisfies that craving for hot and spicy that I sometimes get.

Serves 4

450 grams of fresh lamb mince
5 tablespoons of vegetable oil
2 onions. sliced
2 tablespoons of natural yoghurt
1 teaspoon of chilli powder
1 tablespoon of chopped ginger
1 tablespoon of crushed garlic
1 teaspoon of salt
2 fresh green chillies
2 to 3 tablespoons of fresh coriander leaves
6 cardamom pods
4 cloves
2.5 cm cinnamon stick
2 teaspoons of Nigella seeds
25 grams of ground almonds
25 grams of creamed coconut
1 tablespoon of chopped fresh mint

Pre-heat the oven to 190 degrees C, gas mark 5.

Heat the vegetable oil in a saucepan. Add the onions and fry until golden.

Grind the cardamom, cloves, cinnamon and Nigella seeds in a food processor to form the ground spices.

Place the lamb mince in a bowl. Add the yoghurt, chilli powder, ginger, garlic, salt and ground spices and mix well. Add the fried onions to the lamb mixture.

Meanwhile place the green chillies, the coriander leaves and mint leaves together with the creamed coconut in a food processor and grind. Mix this with the lamb mixture together with the vegetable oil and leave to marinate in a fridge for 2 hours.

For those of you who are really adventurous and wish to achieve the authentic taste of this dish, which is normally cooked in an open flame over hot coals, follow these simple steps while the lamb is marinating in the fridge:

Hold a piece of barbecue coal over a naked flame until it begins to ash and turn grey. Place the smouldering coal on a piece of foil and drizzle oil over the top. Wrap the foil over the coal leaving a small gap at the top through which the smoke and aroma can escape. Place this foil package on top of the mince while it is marinating in the fridge and cover the dish with foil to retain the aroma.

Remove the foil-covered coal package and stir the lamb mixture again. Place it in an oven dish and cook in the oven for 30 to 40 minutes until the meat is tender and fully cooked.

Roast Leg of Lamb

This is a really lavish dish to have carved and ready at the dinner table at times when you really want to impress your guests. I love dressing it up with chopped coriander, lemon wedges, red onion rings and sweet juicy vine cherry tomatoes. Make sure you purchase meat of fine quality as it will absorb the distinct flavours of the marinade. This can be enjoyed with nothing more than a fresh salad and naan.

Serves 4-6

675 gram leg of lamb
6 large cloves of garlic
1 tablespoon of chopped ginger
4 dried red chillies
150 ml of natural yoghurt
2 tablespoons of wine vinegar
2 tablespoons of chopped fresh
    coriander
1 teaspoon of garam masala (refer
    to Glossary)
1/2 teaspoon of ground turmeric
Salt to taste
6 tablespoons of ghee or oil
2 onions, chopped
4 cloves
4 black peppercorns
3 bay leaves
2.5 cm of cinnamon stick
1 black cardamom pod
1 tablespoon ground coriander
1 teaspoon ground roasted cumin
1/2 teaspoon ground turmeric
1/4 teaspoon ground mace
1/4 teaspoon ground nutmeg
400 grams of canned tomatoes
500 ml of water

Garnish
1/2 teaspoon of garam masala
1 tablespoon of fresh coriander
1 small green chilli
Lemon wedges
Sliced red onion

Blend the garlic, ginger, chillies, yoghurt, wine vinegar, coriander, garam masala, turmeric and salt to a smooth paste in a food processor. Rub it over the lamb, having made cuts in the meat to allow the marinade to infuse, cover and leave to marinate for 4 hours.

Heat the ghee or oil in a heavy based pan and fry the onions and whole spices to include the cloves, peppercorns, bay leaves, cinnamon stick and cardamom pod over a medium heat until golden brown.

Stir in the ground spices and then the tomatoes and water and cook until all the liquid has been absorbed and the ghee appears on the surface.

Transfer the marinated lamb to an oven dish together with the marinade and pour the entire contents of the heavy based pan over the lamb. Place the lamb in the oven at 190 degrees C, gas mark 5, for 1 1/4 hours, basting occasionally with ghee or vegetable oil.

Remove the lamb from the oven and reduce the oven temperature to 160 degrees C, gas mark 3. Place the lamb on a large sheet of foil, brush with vegetable oil, then wrap the foil around the meat to enclose it completely. Return to the oven and roast for a further 45 minutes to an hour, or until tender.

Leave the lamb to rest for 10 minutes before carving and serving. Decorate with the garnish ingredients.

Poultry Dishes

At home, I tend to cook different variations of chicken four to five times a week. That is the wonderful thing about chicken. It does not possess a strong taste and, because of this, it takes on the flavour of its surrounding ingredients, so you can never tire of it. My freezer is packed with portions of boneless chicken thigh fillets. It is the tastier part of the bird due to its self-contained succulent moisture. Although my preference is for thigh over breast I am perfectly aware of the fact that breast is the healthier option. The thigh meat has a little bit more fat, but this is compensated for by its having a lot more taste. Chicken is a very convenient meal to prepare because of its versatility and it generally cooks very quickly, which makes it an ideal weekday meal for busy families. If you decide to prepare a saucy curry dish of chicken, then you may decide to purchase a whole bird and prepare the portions yourself with the bone in. The bone contains marrow, which enriches the taste of the curry.

I hope you enjoy trying out the variations in chicken dishes as much as I have enjoyed creating, cooking and eating them!

Barbecued Chicken

To put it simply, this is finger licking delicious. It's an all time favourite Indian starter for all chicken fans. The thought of this dish makes me immediately salivate. It floods my mind with memories of hot summers, barbecuing, with the smell of charcoal smoke all around us. This is an exciting alternative to plain Jane barbecued chicken.

Serves 6

6 portions of thighs and 6 portions
   of drumsticks, skinned
2 tablespoons of chopped ginger
10 cloves of garlic, crushed
1 onion, chopped
300 ml natural yoghurt
2 teaspoons of chilli powder
1 teaspoon of cumin seeds
Salt to taste
150 ml of lemon juice
3 tablespoons of butter, melted
1 teaspoon of garam masala (refer
   to Glossary)

Seasoning
1 cinnamon stick1 bay leaf
8 cloves
7 black peppercorns
3 cardamom pods

Grind together the ginger, garlic and onion and blend to a paste in a food processor. Rub over the chicken and leave to marinate for 5 hours.

Grind together all the seasoning ingredients in an electric grinder into a fine powder. Take out this mixture into a bowl and add the chilli powder, cumin seeds, salt, lemon juice and yoghurt. Mix well.

Make a few slashes on each chicken piece and smear with the mixture. Leave to stand for 1 hour.

Brush the chicken with melted butter and barbecue or grill for about 30 minutes until cooked through thoroughly and browned. Make sure to turn frequently. Sprinkle with garam masala before serving.

Ginger Chicken Chilli Fry

Serves 4

I have adapted this style of chicken, originally a Chinese dish, and made it simply scrumptious. This is one of my signature dishes and is always a hit. Save this for a day when you're ready to fry and the bathroom scales are safely hidden from view. This is one dish I would trade chocolate for.

6 portions of chicken thigh meat,
  cut into small pieces
2 tablespoons of chopped ginger
5 cloves of garlic
5 green chillies
Juice of 1/2 a lemon
Salt and pepper to taste
4 eggs, beaten
100 grams of plain flour (seasoned
  with a little salt and coarsely
  ground black pepper)
Oil for deep frying
2 teaspoons of soya sauce (light)
2 teaspoons Thai sweet chilli sauce
2 tablespoons tamarind pulp (or 1
  tablespoon of tamarind paste)

Place the chicken in a heavy based pan. Just cover with water and bring to boil. Thereafter cover and simmer gently for about 45 minutes until tender. Drain off the water (which you should save and freeze to use as stock another time).

Grind together 1 tablespoon of the ginger, garlic and chillies in a food processor.

Rub the chicken with the lemon then coat with the ground paste and season with salt and pepper.

Dip each of the chicken pieces in egg and then the seasoned flour. Repeat the process of dipping in the egg and the flour once more.

Deep fry the coated chicken pieces until browned and then set aside.

In a wok or heavy based frying pan add 2 tablespoons of oil and fry the remaining 1 tablespoon of ginger. After a minute or so add the soya sauce, Thai sweet chilli sauce and the tamarind sauce. Cook for a minute on a high heat until the mixture is hot and bubbling. By this point the sauce will have caramelised. Add the chicken to the wok and stir fry on a high heat until all the chicken pieces are coated.

Classic Chicken Curry

There are so many different variations of this dish and although I am providing you with a list of ingredients, please feel free to adjust the spices according to your preference as chicken really absorbs the flavour of its surrounding ingredients. This, I must say, is an amazing recipe and once you have your spice collection and you have tried it once or twice, it becomes a breeze to make. I have wowed many guests with this dish and I think it's high time this recipe goes into the public domain.

Serves 4–6

12 chicken pieces, skinned
5 tablespoons of oil or ghee
2 onions, thinly sliced
5 cloves of garlic, chopped
1 tablespoon of chopped ginger
15 cm of cinnamon stick
4 cloves
4 black peppercorns
2 bay leaves
1 black cardamom pod
1 tablespoon of ground aniseeds
1 tablespoon of ground almond
1 tablespoon of ground coriander
1 teaspoon of ground roasted
    cumin
1/2 teaspoon of ground red chilli
1/2 teaspoon of ground turmeric
400 grams of canned tomatoes,
    chopped
Salt to taste
150 ml of natural yoghurt
175 ml of water

Garnish
1/2 teaspoon of garam masala
    (refer to Glossary)
1 tablespoon of chopped fresh
    coriander1 small chilli, chopped

Heat the oil and fry the onions, garlic, ginger and whole spices over a medium heat until golden brown.

Add the chicken and fry until golden brown on all sides.

Stir in the ground spices, tomatoes and salt and cook until all the liquid has been absorbed and the oil appears on the surface.

Add the yoghurt and cook until all the liquid has been absorbed.

Add two thirds of the water, cover and simmer over a low heat for 20 minutes until the chicken is tender, stirring occasionally.

Add the remaining water, increase the heat to medium and cook for a further 2 minutes until the sauce is the consistency that you prefer.

Before serving, garnish by sprinkling garam masala over the top followed by the green chilli and chopped coriander.

Chicken Palak

This is a delicious curried chicken dish made with spinach. Please try to use sweet baby spinach. It's a traditional favourite and as my son said recently, "Popeye would love this dish". It's a sneaky way of getting the kids to eat the greens they usually turn their noses up at.

Serves 4

8 chicken thigh portions, skinned
  (with or without bone)
3 tablespoons of ghee
2 onions, sliced
5 cloves of garlic, crushed
1 tablespoon of chopped ginger
2 cloves
1 teaspoon of ground coriander
2 tomatoes, skinned and chopped
450 grams of baby spinach,
  chopped
Salt and pepper to taste

Heat the ghee and fry the onions until golden brown.

Add the garlic and ginger and cook until soft.

Add the cloves, coriander, tomatoes and spinach and cook for 5 minutes until the spinach is softened and wilted. Season with salt and pepper.

Add the chicken and cover and simmer gently for about 45 minutes until the chicken is tender.

Then turn the heat up to high and continue to cook, stirring constantly, until all the water from the spinach has evaporated.

The chicken can be substituted with lamb but will require more cooking time.

Chicken Dhansak

This is a traditional Parsi dish with lentils. It is traditionally a hot, sweet and sour dish and there are many versions of this curry house favourite, but I think you will agree, once you have tried it, that this version is seriously delicious. The chicken can be substituted for lamb in equal quantity which will require more cooking time.

Serves 4

8 chicken thigh portions, skinned
225 grams of yellow split peas
225 grams of mixed lentils, soaked
1 potato, diced
1 aubergine, diced
2 onions, sliced
3 tablespoons of ghee
1 bunch of fresh fenugreek, finely
    chopped
1 slice of pumpkin, peeled and
    diced (optional)
3 tomatoes, skinned and diced
Salt to taste

Seasoning

1/2 teaspoon of cumin seeds
1/2 teaspoon of ground turmeric
1/2 teaspoon of fenugreek seeds
1/2 teaspoon of mustard seeds
1/2 teaspoon of black pepper
1 teaspoon of chilli powder
2 teaspoons of ground coriander
2 to 3 mint leaves
1 tablespoon of roughly chopped
    ginger
6 cloves of garlic
5 green chillies
2 to 3 tablespoons of chopped
    coriander leaves
2 tablespoons of tamarind pulp (or
    1 tablespoon of tamarind paste)

Soak separately the split peas and lentils for about 2 hours. Drain the split peas and lentils and place in a pan with the chicken, potato, aubergine and 1 onion. Bring to the boil and simmer for about 40 minutes until cooked.

Meanwhile grind all the seasoning ingredients, except the tamarind, to a paste in a food processor.

Heat the ghee and fry the remaining onion and add the ground seasoning ingredients, fenugreek, pumpkin, tomatoes, tamarind and salt.

Remove the meat mixture in Step 1 from the first pan and add to the onion mixture in Step 3 with a little salt and a little more water, only if necessary.

Simmer for 10 minutes until the chicken is cooked and then bring to a high heat and constantly stir the mixture until the oil separates from the curry and comes to the surface.

The chicken can be substituted with lamb but will require more cooking time.

Saffron Chicken

Saffron is the most expensive spice in the world. I obtain my supply from my trusted cousin who lives in Iran. It needs to be of a good quality so you can really appreciate its taste. Saffron not only has a really pleasing flavour but also gives the dish a golden yellow colour. Its aroma is unique and there is no substitute for it. Never buy it in its powdered form, always whole, and crush the threads only just before using. This dish is wonderfully fragrant and spiced, both mouth watering and creamy, is easy to make and extremely satisfying. It's perfect for a cosy night in.

Serves 4

1 chicken skinned and cut into portions with the bone in
1/2 teaspoon of saffron strands
3 tablespoons of hot milk
1 onion, chopped
4 cloves of garlic, chopped
1 tablespoon of chopped ginger
1 green chilli, chopped
3 tablespoons of water
3 tablespoons of oil
Salt to taste
3 teaspoons of garam masala (refer to Glossary)
1 teaspoon of ground cardamom
3 tablespoons of natural yoghurt

Place the saffron in the hot milk for 15 minutes.

Blend the onion, garlic, ginger, chilli and water to a smooth paste.

Heat the oil and fry the paste and salt to taste over a medium heat until the oil appears on the surface.

Add the garam masala and cardamom and cook for 1 minute, stirring.

Whisk the saffron milk into the yoghurt then stir into the pan and cook for 2 minutes.

Remove from the heat and pour the mixture all over the chicken, ensuring all the chicken is covered.

Place in a baking tin, seal tightly with foil and bake in a pre-heated oven at 180 degrees C, gas mark 4, for 45 minutes.

Remove the foil and cook for 15 minutes.

Tandoori Chicken

This ever popular dish is full of flavour. Tempt your taste buds with this hot and juicy recipe. Most of us don't have a tandoor oven. The closest you can achieve to getting the barbecue taste would be using the hot coal technique whilst the meat is marinating. This technique is described in my Oven Baked Minced Lamb (dum ke kheema) recipe in this book. I have managed to perfect the classic version of the recipe for tandoori chicken here, so do away with your ready made paste and give it a go. Ideally, this should be marinated in the fridge overnight, or at least for as long as possible.

Serves 4–6

Either 1 chicken, skinned and
   pricked with a fork or 12 thigh or
   drumstick portions, with the bone,
   slashed
4 tablespoons of lemon juice
6 cloves of garlic
2 tablespoons of chopped ginger
1 onion, coarsely chopped
1 small green chilli
150 ml of natural yoghurt, whisked
1 tablespoon of ground coriander
2 tablespoons of garam masala
   (refer to Glossary)
1 teaspoon of ground roasted
   cumin
1 teaspoon of ground turmeric
1/2 teaspoon of ground red chilli
1/4 teaspoon of ground mace
1/4 teaspoon of grated nutmeg
Salt to taste
5 tablespoons of melted ghee or
   butter

Garnish
1 teaspoon of garam masala
1 onion, cut into rings
1 lemon, sliced
2 tablespoons of chopped fresh
   coriander
1 small green chilli, chopped

Blend the lemon juice, garlic, ginger, onion and chilli to a smooth paste in a blender or food processor.

Place the yoghurt, ground spices, nutmeg and salt in a bowl and stir in the paste.

Put the chicken into the marinade and rub it all over with the marinade. Cover and leave to marinate overnight or for as long as possible.

Place two skewers through the marinated whole chicken and put the chicken in a deep ovenproof dish, resting the skewers on the top of the dish so that the chicken is not touching the bottom of the dish. Alternatively, use the same method if you are using chicken thigh portions or drumsticks, supporting the portions with the long skewers in the same way.

Roast in a pre-heated oven at 180 degrees C, gas mark 4, for about 2 hours until the chicken is tender, turning and basting with the marinade and the melted ghee as it cooks. This will take approximately 1 hour if you are making it with chicken thigh portions or drumsticks.

Transfer the chicken to a serving dish, garnish with the garnish ingredients before serving.

Curried Chicken Livers

This is so delicious even for those who don't like chicken livers. I have to say chicken liver has never been high on my agenda but it's different from other livers in that it doesn't get tough with excess cooking. Also, it contains many more vitamins, minerals and essential nutrients gram for gram than any other food. Be aware, however, that it's quite high in cholesterol. This dish is very tender and equally delicious.

Serves 4

450 grams of chicken livers
150 ml of natural yoghurt
2 onions, sliced
6 cloves of garlic
1 tablespoon of roughly chopped ginger
2 celery sticks, chopped
2 tablespoons of ghee or vegetable oil
6 cloves
2 cinnamon sticks
2 cardamom pods
1 teaspoon of ground turmeric
2 green chillies, chopped
Salt to taste
20 curry leaves

Chop the liver into 2.5 cm pieces and leave to marinate in the yoghurt.

Blend 1 onion, the garlic, ginger and celery to a paste.

Heat the ghee or oil and fry the cloves, cinnamon and cardamom for 2 minutes.

Add to these spices the turmeric, curry leaves, salt and chillies and fry for about 15 minutes until browned.

Add the liver and remaining onion and simmer over a low heat for about 10 minutes until the liver is cooked and the sauce is thickened.

Chicken Tikka

Serves 6

The word "tikka" means pieces or chunks. This is the authentic recipe. There is no skimping on taste here. This takeaway favourite is freezer-friendly and quick to re-heat, giving you a chance to get ahead in the busy week. This goes into the category of Indian-inspired barbecue food (although it turns out really well cooked under the grill too). It's perfect as a finger food snack at a cocktail party with a mint yoghurt dip or even as a main meal with grilled onions and peppers and a fresh naan bread. It's ideal for when it's too hot for a curry but you still fancy a bit of spice. If possible, try and marinate the chicken overnight.

1.5 kilograms or 12 boneless portions of thigh meat, skinned and cut into chunks
1 tablespoon of chopped ginger
1 tablespoon of garlic cloves, crushed
1/2 teaspoon of ground coriander
1/2 teaspoon of ground cumin
1 teaspoon of chilli powder
150 ml of natural yoghurt
1 teaspoon of salt
2 tablespoons of lemon juice
Red food colouring (optional)
1 tablespoon of tomato puree
1 onion, sliced
3 tablespoons of vegetable oil

Blend the ginger, garlic, ground coriander, cumin and chilli powder together in a large bowl. Add the yoghurt, salt, lemon juice, red food colouring (if using) and tomato puree to the spice mixture.

Add the chicken to the spice mixture and toss to coat well. Cover and leave to marinate in the refrigerator for at least 3 hours, preferably overnight.

Pre-heat the grill to medium. Arrange the onion in the base of a large heat-proof dish. Carefully drizzle half the vegetable oil over the onions.

Arrange the marinated chicken pieces on top of the onions and cook under the pre-heated grill, turning once and basting with the remaining oil, for 25 to 30 minutes.

Butter Chicken (Murgh Makhani)

This rich, mild dish can be tracked back to Moghul times. It's one of the best known Indian foods all over the world. It has been tried and tested a great many times and loved by everyone who has eaten it. This is my recipe for butter chicken, as it's the real deal. If possible, marinate the chicken overnight.

Serves 6

6 chicken breasts or large bone-
    less thigh portions, skinned
150 ml natural yoghurt
1 tablespoon of crushed ginger
Salt to taste
55 grams of butter
1 cinnamon stick
6 cardamom pods
6 cloves
2 bay leaves
150 ml of sour cream
150 ml of single cream
Large pinch of saffron thread,
    crushed
1 tablespoon of ground almonds
1/4 teaspoon of cornflour

Mix the yoghurt, ginger and 1 teaspoon of salt in a large, shallow dish.

Cut each chicken portion into 3 pieces and add to the dish.

Rub the yoghurt mixture into the chicken, and cover with clingfilm and leave to marinate in the refrigerator, preferably overnight, but at the very least for an hour.

Remove the chicken from the dish, reserving any marinade.

Melt the butter in a large, heavy based frying pan, add the chicken and cook over a low heat, turning occasionally for about 10 minutes or until browned and nearly cooked through. Remove with a slotted spoon and reserve.

Add the cinnamon, cardamoms, cloves and bay leaves to the frying pan and cook, stirring constantly, for about 1 minute, or until they give off their aroma.

Add the reserved marinade, sour cream, single cream and saffron and stir well, then cover and simmer for about 5 minutes.

Return the chicken pieces to the frying pan and stir in the ground almonds.

Mix the cornflour with enough water to make a smooth paste and stir into the saucepan.

Cover and simmer for 5 minutes or until the chicken is tender and cooked through. Taste and add more salt, if necessary.

Seafood Dishes

The fish purchased in India are very different from those available elsewhere, so these recipes have been adapted to suit western species of fish. Fish is one of the most versatile ingredients and is equally delicious as spicy curries, creamy stews or presented as fragrantly marinated kebabs. There are recipes for both freshwater and sea fish, as well as great ways of cooking prawns.

Fish Curry

This makes for a perfect dinner on a hot night in that it's light enough not to knock you out, but spiced enough to prompt a heat-drowsy appetite, combined with the fact that it's gloriously easy to make.

4 large garlic cloves
2 onions, cut into chunks
1 tablespoon of chopped ginger
50 ml of wine vinegar
500 grams of cod or haddock
   fillets cut into 5-cm pieces
90 ml or 6 tablespoons of oil

Sauce:
4 tablespoons of oil
1 teaspoon of mustard seeds
1 onion, finely chopped
4 cloves
4 peppercorns
2 bay leaves
1 black cardamom pod
1.5 cm cinnamon stick
1 teaspoon of ground roasted
   cumin
1 teaspoon of ground turmeric
1/2 teaspoon of ground red chilli
Salt to taste
225 grams of canned tomatoes
170 ml (two-thirds of a cup) of
   natural yoghurt
1 tablespoon of sugar
250 ml or 1 cup of water

Garnish
1 teaspoon garam masala (refer to
   Glossary)
1 tablespoon of chopped fresh
   coriander
1 small chopped chilli

Puree the garlic, onions, ginger and wine vinegar to a smooth paste in a blender or food processor.

Marinate the fish in half the paste for 30 minutes. Reserve the other half for the sauce.

Make the sauce while the fish is marinating. Heat the oil in a heavy based pan and fry the mustard seeds until they start crackling.

Add the onion and whole spices and fry until golden brown.

Mix in the reserved paste and fry for a few minutes until golden brown.

Stir in the ground spices and salt and then tomatoes and cook until all the liquid has been absorbed.

Add the yoghurt and sugar and cook again until all the liquid has been absorbed and the oil appears on the surface.

Add the water, bring to boil then simmer over a low heat for 5 minutes.

Meanwhile, heat the 90 ml of oil and fry the fish over a medium heat for 15 minutes until light brown, turning once or twice. Remove from the pan and place on a serving dish.

Pour the sauce over the fish, and sprinkle with the garnish ingredients.

Mughal-style Fish Curry in Almond Sauce

Serves 6

This is a rich fish curry. The combination of spices brings just the right level of heat and flavour to this lavish dish. This delicately prepared dish has an amazingly unique flavour so please don't be put off by the long list of ingredients because it will be worth every minute you spend making it.

2 large portions of plaice cut into
   5cm pieces
1 tablespoon of chopped ginger
6 cloves of garlic
Salt to taste
1 tablespoon black mustard seeds
Juice of 1 lemon
3 tablespoons of oil
1 large onion, chopped
3 tablespoons of hot water
1/4 cup of blanched almonds
2 tablespoons of coriander seeds
2 teaspoons of cumin seeds
2 dried red chillies
1 teaspoon of ground turmeric
1/2 teaspoon of saffron threads
3 tablespoons of hot milk
6 cardamom pods
1 cinnamon stick
1/2 teaspoon of black peppercorns
2 bay leaves
1/4 teaspoon of cloves
3 tablespoons of natural yoghurt

Blend the ginger, garlic, salt, mustard seeds and lemon juice in a blender or food processor and then spread the puree over and into the fish. Leave to marinate in the fridge for 3 hours.

Heat the oil and fry the onion until soft.

Puree the water, almonds, coriander and cumin seeds, chillies and turmeric in a blender or pestle and mortar.

Dissolve the saffron in the hot milk and leave to soak for 15 minutes.

Stir the cardamom, cinnamon, peppercorns, bay leaves and cloves into the onions and cook for 2 minutes.

Add the pureed spices and cook for 6 to 8 minutes, stirring constantly, until the oil appears on the surface.

Lightly whisk the saffron milk and yoghurt together with a fork then stir into the pan and simmer for 2 minutes.

Put the fish into a casserole dish and pour over the sauce. Bake in a pre-heated oven at 180 degrees C, gas mark 4, for 15 minutes until the fish is cooked and the sauce starts bubbling.

Fish Kofta Curry

Serves 4

This is basically fish balls in a delicious thick gravy. This is quite light and therefore makes a perfect lunch or dinner. It goes perfectly well with either rice or a green salad, or a dry vegetarian side dish.

100 grams of boneless white fish fillets. chopped
2 medium onions. chopped
1/2 cup (firmly packed) or 5 tablespoons of fresh coriander leaves
2 large fresh red chillies. chopped
1 tablespoon ghee or butter
2 cloves of garlic. crushed
2 teaspoons of ground coriander
1 teaspoon of ground cumin
1/2 teaspoon of ground turmeric
2 cinnamon sticks
1 teaspoon of ground fenugreek
3 medium tomatoes. peeled and chopped
Salt to taste

Bring a large pan of water to the boil and then add the fish. Simmer, uncovered, until the fish is tender.

Remove from the heat and strain the fish over a large bowl. Reserve 2 cups or 500 ml of the liquid.

Blend the fish in a food processor with one onion, half the fresh coriander and both of the chillies until just combined.

Shape the koftas into either round or oval shaped balls, a tablespoon of mixture for each, and place on a tray. Refrigerate for 30 minutes.

Heat half the ghee or butter in a non-stick frying pan and fry the koftas until browned on both sides. Then set aside.

Heat the remaining ghee or butter in a large pan and cook the remaining onion, the garlic and all spices, stirring, until the onion is browned lightly. Add the tomatoes and continue stirring for about 5 minutes or until the tomatoes are very soft. Add the reserved liquid and simmer, uncovered, for about 10 minutes or until the sauce is thickened.

Add the koftas and simmer for 5 minutes or until the koftas are heated through. Just before serving sprinkle with the remaining coriander.

Marinated Fish

Serves 4

Pep up your taste buds with this relishable dish. Try serving it with mixed long grain basmati rice and wild rice grains with finely chopped coriander stirred in. It always looks very appealing served on a dish dressed up with lots of garnish. It's very simple to make but has the desired effect of wowing your guests.

4 red mullet (alternatively you can use snapper or sea bass) in the whole form and clean
1 fresh green chilli
125 ml of lime juice
4 tablespoons of natural yoghurt
1 teaspoon of garlic paste (refer to Glossary)
1 teaspoon of ginger paste (refer to Glossary)
1 tablespoon of coriander seeds
1 teaspoon of garam masala (refer to Glossary)
A few drops of red food colouring (optional)
85 grams of butter
2 teaspoons of ground cumin
Salt to taste
Lime wedges and fresh coriander sprigs to garnish

De-seed and chop the green chilli and reserve.

Using a sharp knife, slash the fish diagonally several times on both sides and sprinkle with lime juice.

Place the yoghurt, garlic paste, ginger paste, coriander seeds, chopped chilli and garam masala in a food processor and make a paste. Transfer to a shallow dish and stir in the red food colouring (although I have said that this is optional).

Add the fish, turning to coat. Cover with clingfilm and leave to marinate in the refrigerator for 8 hours, turning occasionally.

Pre-heat the oven to 190 degrees C, gas mark 5. Remove the fish from the marinade and place on a rack in a roasting tin. Cook in a pre-heated oven for 10 minutes.

Meanwhile, melt the butter in a small saucepan over a low heat. Do not let the butter turn brown when you are doing this, otherwise it will taste bitter and may spoil the finished dish. Remove the saucepan from the heat and stir in the cumin.

Brush the butter all over the fish and return to the oven for a further 6 to 7 minutes, or until cooked through.

Garnish with lime wedges and fresh coriander when serving.

Indian Spiced Trout with Ginger

This is a lightly grilled golden brown trout which is very flavourful. Leave the trout in its whole form and it will look quite spectacular when it's served with the garnish. Young, tender ginger, which has translucent skin and pink tips, is best for this dish, but please don't worry if you can't get hold of this.

Serves 4

4 trout cleaned
1 teaspoon ginger paste (refer to Glossary)
1 teaspoon garlic paste (refer to Glossary)
2 fresh green chillies, de-seeded and finely chopped
1 tablespoon of chopped fresh coriander
1/4 teaspoon of ground turmeric
Salt and pepper to taste
Vegetable oil for brushing
Fresh coriander sprigs and lime slices to garnish

Pre-heat the grill to medium. Mix the ginger paste, garlic paste, fresh chillies, coriander, turmeric, 1 teaspoon of pepper and a pinch of salt together in a small bowl. Stir in enough water to make a smooth paste.

Using a sharp knife, slash the trout diagonally on both sides two or three times. Rub the paste into the fish, especially the slashes.

Brush with vegetable oil and cook under the pre-heated grill for 15 minutes, turning once and brushing with more vegetable oil. Garnish with coriander sprigs and lime slices just before serving.

Monkfish Kebabs

Serves 4

This fish is marinated in a delicious mixture of herbs, spices and lime juice before being threaded onto skewers together with a selection of colourful vegetables. You can substitute the monkfish with large, raw, peeled prawns with their tails left intact if you like.

350 grams of monkfish, cubed
3 tablespoons of lime juice
1 tablespoon of finely chopped
   fresh mint
1 tablespoon of finely chopped
   fresh coriander
2 fresh green chillies, de-seeded
   and finely chopped
1 teaspoon of ginger paste
1/2 teaspoon of garlic paste
1 teaspoon of ground coriander
   seeds
Salt to taste
1 red pepper, de-seeded and cut
   into chunks
1 green pepper, de-seeded and cut
   into chunks
8 button mushrooms
8 cherry tomatoes
1 tablespoon of sunflower oil
Lime wedges and fresh coriander
   sprigs to garnish

Mix the lime juice, mint, fresh coriander, chillies, ginger paste, garlic paste, ground coriander and a pinch of salt together in a large shallow and non-metallic dish. Add the fish and stir to coat. Cover with clingfilm and leave to marinate in a cool place for 30 minutes. If you will be using wooden or bamboo skewers, soak them in a bowl of warm water while the fish is marinating to prevent them charring under the grill.

Pre-heat the grill to medium. Drain the fish and reserve the marinade. Thread the monkfish and the peppers, mushrooms and tomatoes onto the skewers.

Brush the kebabs with any remaining marinade and the sunflower oil and cook under the pre-heated grill, turning and basting frequently, for about 10 minutes or until cooked. Garnish with lime wedges and coriander sprigs when ready to serve.

Bombay Prawns

The original dish may have changed its name a couple of times, but the recipe has always remained the same. What can I say? All prawn lovers that I know of, are devoted to this fabulously tasty dish, especially those who feel like something with a bit of spice.

1 kilogram raw tiger prawns, cleaned, peeled and de-veined
2 fresh green chillies, de-seeded and chopped
400 grams of canned tomatoes
4 tablespoons of tomato puree
55 grams of dark brown sugar
1 tablespoon of lemon juice
5 tablespoons of fresh coriander leaves, plus extra to garnish
2 tablespoons of ghee or vegetable oil
2 onions, chopped
1 teaspoon of garlic paste (refer to Glossary)
2 teaspoons of ground cumin
2 teaspoons of garam masala (refer to Glossary)
2 teaspoons of ground coriander
1 teaspoon of chilli powder
1 teaspoon of ground turmeric
6 curry leaves
Salt to taste

Place the chillies, tomatoes, tomato puree, sugar, lemon juice and coriander leaves in the food processor and make a paste.

Heat the ghee in a large, heavy based saucepan. Add the onions and cook over a low heat, stirring occasionally for about 10 minutes or until they are golden.

Stir in the garlic paste, cumin, garam masala, ground coriander, chilli powder and turmeric and cook for a further 2 minutes, or until the spices give off their aroma.

Increase the heat, stir in the tomato mixture and curry leaves, add salt to taste and bring to the boil. Reduce the heat and simmer for about 10 minutes or until the mixture is slightly thickened.

Add the prawns and stir to coat well in the sauce. Simmer for a further 6 to 8 minutes, or until they change colour. Garnish with coriander before serving.

Vegetarian Dishes

I have a family of carnivores so I never really concentrated my efforts on perfecting my vegetarian eclectic pallet. In an attempt to be healthy I used to occasionally and optimistically present vegetarian dishes to discerning family faces and the meal generally went down like a lead balloon. I stood more chance of playing golf on the moon than getting them to eat anything vegetarian other than my "khuti dhal" – a Hyderabadi favourite, and a guaranteed cure for blocked sinuses!

That is, until I decided to concentrate my culinary efforts on perfecting the art of making vegetarian Indian food. Don't give me too much credit – I am not there yet. What I can tell you is that I have collected and transcribed all the recipes from friends and family who have perfected this art to a fine tee.

Vegetarian Indian food is underrated in western society, which is surprising being that the majority of Indians don't eat meat and therefore have the world's richest and most varied vegetarian dishes. I will show you how to do a complete makeover on the most humble of vegetables, such as potato, spinach and cauliflower, with wonderful medleys, creamy combinations and both mild and fiery flavours with an amazing array of colours. Take my word for it – once you have identified and developed a taste for these spices, you will be adding them to your veggies at every opportunity.

Punjabi-style Aubergine Curry

I challenge all aubergine detesters to try this because it will change your opinion of this underrated vegetable forever. This is a simple and tasty vegetarian Indian dish that is sure to rouse your taste buds. It's delicious served on its own or as an accompaniment to a meat curry along with fresh naan or rice.

Serves 4

450 grams of aubergine, cubed and then boiled for 10 mins until tender
65ml or 1/4 cup of ghee or vegetable oil
Pinch of cumin seeds
1 onion, chopped
2 cloves of garlic, chopped
1 tablespoon of finely grated ginger
2 tomatoes, skinned and quartered
Salt to taste
2 green chillies, chopped
1/2 teaspoon of garam masala (refer to Glossary)
1 tablespoon of chopped fresh coriander

Heat the ghee or oil and fry the cumin seeds, onion, garlic and ginger for 2 minutes.

Add the tomatoes, aubergine, salt and chillies and cook for 10 minutes, stirring continuously.

Turn onto a high heat and continue to stir continuously until all the liquid is absorbed.

Sprinkle with a little garam masala and fresh coriander to garnish before serving.

Okra with Cumin and Garlic

I have always felt that okra (which is also known as "ladies' fingers" as clearly there wasn't a manicurist in sight when this vegetable was so named) is a really underrated vegetable. It seems as if people don't really know what to do with okra. It's such a versatile vegetable – there are so many ways to prepare okra in Indian cuisine and I love them all. They can be sautéed, fried or even stuffed. You name it, it exists. Okra contains a good amount of protein, but it has the unfortunate problem of appearing slimy. Always wash it thoroughly when it's in its whole form, but ensure each okra is dried fully, using kitchen roll, before it's cut. When the slime appears during cooking, just continue to cook it out and it should disappear. This always makes the perfect dry vegetarian side dish to a saucy meat curry.

Serves 6

15 kilograms of okra
3 tablespoons of oil
1 onion, chopped
10 cloves of garlic, chopped
2 green chillies, chopped
1 teaspoon of turmeric
1 tablespoon of ground cumin
Salt to taste

Prepare the okra by washing thoroughly and allowing to dry on absorbent paper or a clean kitchen towel.

Heat the oil and fry the onion, garlic and chillies until browned.

Stir in the turmeric and cumin and fry for 2 minutes until the oil appears on the surface.

Stir in the okra and salt to taste, cover and simmer gently for 8 to 10 minutes until the okra is tender, stirring occasionally.

Stuffed Okra

This is one of the best vegetarian recipes of all time with its origins in Gujarat. I am not exaggerating when I tell you it is out of this world. Those who hate okra will definitely fall in love with it once they have tried this dish. Be sure the okra is tender and fresh and that you put a good amount of stuffing in each one; the combination of ingredients that goes into the stuffing is extremely flavourful so don't skimp on the quantity in each okra. This is a perfect accompaniment to plain steamed rice and a dhal of your choice. Making sure you dry the okra very well before stuffing them and then searing them when stuffed on a high heat initially will prevent them from getting slimy.

Serves 4

225 grams of okra, slit
4 tablespoons of ghee
2 tablespoons of chopped onion
1 tablespoon of coriander seeds, crushed
1/2 teaspoon of grated ginger
Pinch of turmeric
Pinch of chilli powder
Salt to taste
2 teaspoons of lemon juice

Carefully remove the pulp from the okra.

Heat 1 tablespoon of ghee and fry the onion until golden brown.

Stir in the coriander, ginger, turmeric, chilli powder and salt with the okra pulp and cook for 5 minutes. Stir in the lemon juice and then remove from the heat.

Stuff the okra shells with the mixture once it has cooled down.

Heat the remaining ghee in a large frying pan, fry the stuffed okra on a high heat for about 2 minutes initially to sear them and then carefully on a lower heat for a further 10 minutes until tender.

Benares-Style Cauliflower and Potato (also known as Aloo Gobi)

So how many of you watched Bend it Like Beckham *and wondered how to make this classic dish that poor Jess was being hounded by her mother to learn in order to qualify for the making of a good Indian wife? I have chosen the Benari style of making this dish as, having tried so many different variations, I think it is the most flavoursome recipe. Benares is a city on the banks of the Ganges and is the holiest of the seven sacred cities in Hinduism and Jainism. This dish takes seasoning to a new level and the hot spice mix paired with fresh and favourable cauliflower makes for a stunning burst of flavours.*

Serves 6

1 cauliflower, cut into florets
2 large potatoes, cubed
250 ml of water
1 onion, chopped
6 cloves of garlic, chopped
1 tablespoon of chopped ginger
1 tablespoon of coriander seeds
2 tablespoons of oil
1 teaspoon of cumin seeds
1 teaspoon of caraway seeds
1 tablespoon of garam masala
    (refer to Glossary)
1 teaspoon of ground turmeric
Salt to taste

Blend 45 ml, or 3 tablespoons, of the water with the onion, garlic, ginger and coriander to a paste in a food processor.

Heat the oil and fry the cumin and caraway seeds for 1 minute.

Add the puree and fry for 6 minutes, stirring continuously, until the oil appears in the surface,

Mix in the garam masala and turmeric and stir for 30 seconds.

Add the cauliflower, potatoes, salt and remaining water and bring to the boil. Then cover and simmer for 8 to 10 minutes until the vegetables are tender, stirring occasionally.

Tip:
This goes so well with hot chapatis or paratha if you're feeling really indulgent.

Spicy Potatoes

This is a popular Punjabi dish and is really quick to whip up, taking not much longer than 10 minutes to make. The poor photographer for this book struggled to take a picture of this as the potatoes would vanish, as if by magic (or greedy children in my case), before the picture could be taken. This is a great dish to serve as an appetiser, snack or side dish. They go particularly well with gently fried eggs for breakfast.

Serves 4–6

500 grams of potatoes
120 ml of ghee or vegetable oil
1 small onion, finely chopped
4 cloves
4 peppercorns
2 bay leaves
1 cardamom pod
1 cm of cinnamon stick
1 large onion, cut into chunks
2 cloves of garlic
1 tablespoon of coarsely chopped ginger
2 teaspoons of ground coriander
1/2 teaspoon of ground roasted cumin
1/2 teaspoon of ground red chilli
1/2 teaspoon of turmeric
Salt to taste
400 grams of canned tomatoes
150 ml of natural yoghurt
200 ml of water

Garnish
1 tablespoon of chopped fresh coriander
1/2 teaspoon of garam masala (refer to Glossary)
1 small green chilli, chopped

Peel the potatoes and then cut them into small cubes

Heat half the ghee or oil and fry the potatoes until golden brown on all sides. Drain and set aside.

Heat the remaining oil in a heavy based pan and fry the chopped onion, cloves, peppercorns, bay leaves, cardamom and cinnamon over a medium heat until golden brown.

Blend the onion, garlic and ginger to a smooth paste in a food processor.

Stir this mixture into the pan and fry until golden brown.

Stir in the coriander, cumin, chilli, turmeric and salt.

Stir in the tomatoes and cook until the ghee appears on top of the mixture.

Stir in the yoghurt and cook until all of the liquid has been absorbed.

Add the water and fried potatoes. Bring to the boil then cover and cook gently for about 20 minutes until tender.

Sprinkle over the garnish ingredients before serving.

Tandoori Potatoes

Serves 4

Experience with food over the last several years tells me that people love potatoes, especially the dry roasted crispy kind. Easy to prepare and delicious to eat, these can be served as a starter or part of a main course. They are so simple and a flavoursome addition to the table. I often decorate my dish of Tandoori chicken pieces with these potatoes arranged around the perimeter and topped with fresh coriander and thin slices of red onion.

450 grams of potatoes
150 ml of natural yoghurt
3 tablespoons of oil
1 tablespoon of lemon juice
1 clove of garlic. crushed
1 teaspoon of grated ginger
2 green chillies. chopped
1 tablespoon of chopped fresh mint
1 tablespoon of chopped fresh
   coriander
1 teaspoon of garam masala (refer
   to Glossary)
1 teaspoon of ground cumin
1 teaspoon of ground turmeric
1 teaspoon of salt
3 tablespoons of ghee
1 teaspoon of mustard seeds
1 teaspoon of cumin seeds
3 tablespoons of tomato puree

Peel the potatoes and then cut them into small cubes and place in a bowl

Mix together the yoghurt, oil, lemon juice, garlic, ginger, chillies, spices and salt. Stir into the potatoes then cover and marinate overnight or at the very least for a couple of hours in the fridge.

Heat the ghee and fry the mustard seeds and cumin seeds until they start crackling.

Add the tomato puree, potatoes and marinade. Bring to a gentle simmer then cover and simmer for about 15 minutes until the potatoes are tender and the sauce has thickened.

Garnish with the coriander and mint leaves.

Marrow Kofta Curry

I remember trying this for the first time in a popular Indian tapas restaurant in my home town. It was a dish that was ordered by one of my friends. It would never have occurred to me to order it but, being the person that has to try every dish on the table without fail, I have to say this was an unexpected delight. It makes an excellent main dish if you are making a purely vegetarian meal.

Serves 4 (16 koftas)

900 grams of marrow
6 1/2 tablespoons of water
50 grams of gram flour
1/2 teaspoon of garam masala
  (refer to Glossary)
1/2 teaspoon of ground roasted
  cumin
1/2 teaspoon of ground red chillies
1/4 teaspoon of ground mace
1/4 teaspoon of grated (or ground)
  nutmeg
Salt to taste
25 grams of blanched almonds
25 grams of cashew nuts
50 grams of raisins
Oil for deep frying

Sauce

5 tablespoons of ghee or oil
1 small onion, finely chopped
4 large cloves of garlic, crushed
1 tablespoon of coarsely chopped
  ginger
1 onion, coarsely chopped
1 teaspoon of garam masala
1 teaspoon of ground coriander
1 teaspoon of ground roasted
  cumin
1/2 teaspoon of ground red chilli
1/2 teaspoon of ground turmeric
Salt to taste
225 grams of canned tomatoes,
  chopped
150 ml of natural yoghurt
3 tablespoons of water

Peel and grate the marrow. Cook the marrow in the water for about 15 minutes until tender. Drain, reserving the cooking water. Place the marrow in a strainer and press out all the water with the palm of your hand.

Lightly brown the gram flour in a dry frying pan (skillet) on a low heat.

Put the marrow in a bowl and stir in the gram flour, garam masala, cumin, chilli, mace, nutmeg and salt.

Divide the mixture into 16 equal portions.

Flatten each portion and place an almond, a cashew nut and a few raisins in the middle. Bring the edges over to cover and shape into a round ball.

Meanwhile, heat the oil in a deep frying pan, then slip the koftas into the oil and fry until golden brown. Remove with a slotted spoon and put to one side.

To make the sauce, heat the ghee or oil in a heavy based pan and fry the small chopped onion over a medium heat until golden brown.

Blend the garlic, ginger and coarsely chopped onion to a smooth paste in a food processor.

Add to the pan and fry for a few minutes until golden brown.

Stir in the garam masala, coriander, cumin, chilli, turmeric and salt.

Stir in the tomatoes and cook until all the water has been absorbed and the ghee appears on the surface.

Add the yoghurt and cook until all the liquid has been absorbed.

Add the water and cook until all the liquid has been absorbed.

Make up the reserved marrow cooking liquid to 250 ml with water, if necessary. Add to the pan, and bring to the boil, then simmer for a further 2 minutes.

Pour over the koftas.

Spicy Spinach (Saag)

Saag or palak dishes are spiced purees of spinach or other greens common in North India. The flavour of this dish is rich, fragrant and mellow – not hot. Saag and hot parathas are a marriage made in heaven and you reach a point where life doesn't get much better. Spinach releases a lot of water when it is sautéed so dry the leaves well after washing in order to keep the water to a minimum.

Serves 6

1.5 kilograms of baby spinach, washed and chopped
3 turnips, peeled and cubed
450 ml of water
3 tablespoons of oil
1 tablespoon of black mustard seeds
1 onion, chopped
5 cloves of garlic, chopped
1 tablespoon of chopped ginger
1 teaspoon of ground turmeric
1/2 teaspoon of chilli powder
1 tablespoon of garam masala (refer to Glossary)
Salt to taste

Boil the turnips in the water for about 12 minutes until tender then drain and mash.

Heat the oil and fry the mustard seeds until they start crackling.

Stir in the onion, garlic and ginger and cook until brown. Add the turmeric and the chilli powder, garam masala and salt and fry for 1 minute, stirring. Then add the spinach and continue to stir for a further minute.

Stir in the mashed turnips, then cover and simmer for 5 minutes, stirring occasionally.

Then turn the heat up high and constantly stir the mixture until all the water has evaporated.

Chickpea Curry

Serves 4–6

Every year I would make a huge pot of hot chickpea curry for the school summer fete. If I had a penny for every person who asked me for the recipe, I would be writing this book in my Beverly Hills mansion. There are probably as many recipes for this dish as there are households in North India, where this dish originates. This recipe has been tried and tested over the years of summer fetes, and I swear by it.

250 grams of chickpeas, soaked overnight. Alternatively, 250 grams of tinned cooked chickpeas
1/2 teaspoon of bicarbonate of soda (baking soda)
1.75 litres of water
Salt to taste
6 tablespoons of ghee or vegetable oil
1 small onion, finely chopped
4 cloves
4 peppercorns
2 bay leaves
1 cm of cinnamon stick
2 black cardamom pods
4 cloves of garlic
1 tablespoon of coarsely chopped ginger
1 large onion, coarsely chopped
3 tablespoons of water
1 teaspoon of ground coriander
1 teaspoon of ground roasted cumin
1/2 teaspoon of garam masala (refer to Glossary)
1/2 teaspoon of ground red chilli
1/2 teaspoon of ground turmeric
1/4 teaspoon of ground mace
1/4 teaspoon of grated (or ground) nutmeg
400 grams of canned tomatoes

If you have used the chickpeas that required soaking overnight then place these chickpeas in a large pan with the bicarbonate of soda, water and salt. Bring to the boil, skim off any scum, cover and simmer gently for 1 hour until the chickpeas are tender. If you are using the canned version then these will be pre-cooked. Strain the liquid off.

Meanwhile, heat the ghee or oil in a heavy based pan and fry the onion, cloves, peppercorns, bay leaves, cinnamon and cardamom until golden brown.

Blend the garlic, ginger, onion and the 3 tablespoons of water to a smooth paste in a food processor.

Add this paste to the pan and fry for a few minutes until golden brown.

Stir in the coriander, cumin, garam masala, chilli, turmeric, mace, nutmeg and salt to taste. Stir in the tomatoes and simmer until all the liquid has been absorbed and the ghee appears on the surface of the mixture.

Strain the chickpeas then mix them into the sauce and simmer until the chickpeas are thorough tender and have absorbed the flavours of the sauce.

Turn up the heat to high and stir the mixture constantly until the sauce has reduced to the required consistency.

Chilli Paneer

There are so many different versions of this dish. There used to be a popular Indian restaurant situated just across the road from the court house where my fellow lawyers would congregate at lunchtime and devour in the limited time available to us a dish of chilli paneer and fresh tandoori naan. We might have had differences of opinion in court, but we certainly agreed on one thing – that this was the best chilli paneer to be had. I used every drop of charm I have to persuade the chef of this restaurant to reveal this recipe. He did so, in confidence. What can I say, some secrets are destined to be shared. Lesson to be learnt – never trust a lawyer!

Serves 4

225 grams of paneer, diced (refer to Glossary)
Oil for deep frying
1 tablespoon of finely chopped ginger
2 tablespoons of oil
2 teaspoons of light soya sauce
2 teaspoons of Thai sweet chilli sauce
1 tablespoon of tomato hot sauce
1 tablespoon of tamarind pulp
20 whole curry leaves

To make the tamarind pulp, take 2 tablespoons of dried tamarind and boil it for 15 minutes over a medium heat. Rub the tamarind through your fingers to reduce it to a pulp then rub through a sieve and collect the pulp. Discard the husks. Excess pulp can be frozen.

Deep fry the cubes of paneer until golden brown. Remove with a slotted spoon and set aside to drain.

In a heavy based frying pan, karai or wok heat the 2 tablespoons of oil. Then add the ginger and fry on a medium to high heat for about 1 minute. Then add the soya sauce, the Thai sweet chilli sauce, the tomato hot sauce and the tamarind pulp. Increase the heat to high and continue to cook, stirring constantly, until the oil rises to the top of the mixture.

Add the paneer and fold this into the sauce on a medium to high heat for about 3 to 4 minutes to allow the sauces to be absorbed into the paneer. Add the curry leaves and cook for a further 2 minutes. The consistency of this dish should be dry but sticky.

Dhal Makhani

Every month I get together with a couple of school mums with the intention of doing a session of home zumba to a DVD. What actually happens is a paratha and makhani dhal breakfast. This is rich, creamy and luscious and literally translates as "butter dhal". The creamy lentils cooked with the absorbed spices and, of course, butter (which you must not skimp on no matter how much you like zumba) make it one of the best warm soul foods ever.

Serves 4

100 grams of urid dhal (black lentils or black gram)
100 grams of Bengal gram (or another 100 grams of black lentils if this is not available)
100 grams of red kidney beans
5 tablespoons of sunflower oil
1 onion, finely chopped
4 tomatoes, skinned and chopped
Salt to taste
2 tablespoons of ginger that has been cut into very thin strands
2 cloves of garlic, mashed
2 teaspoons of ground coriander
2 teaspoons of ground cumin
1/2 teaspoon of fenugreek seeds, ground
50 grams of butter (unsalted)
180 ml of single cream (save a little to drizzle over the top to garnish)
2 green chillies, chopped
Coriander leaves to garnish

Soak the pulses overnight and then boil together in salted water until cooked. Drain and save the water.

Heat the sunflower oil in a heavy based pan and fry the onion until golden brown.

Add the tomatoes, salt, ginger, garlic, ground coriander, cumin and fenugreek seeds and cook for a further 2 minutes, stirring continuously, until the oil comes to the surface.

Add the pulses and stir into the mixture for 2 to 3 minutes, making sure not to mash the pulses.

Add about 100 ml of the reserved water and cook for a further 5 minutes.

Add the butter, cream and green chilli and continue to cook for 15 minutes on a low to medium heat. The consistency should be thick and soupy.

Garnish with a circle of cream and chopped coriander leaves before serving.

Tarka Dhal

This is also known as masoor dhal. It is a popular restaurant dhal that goes with just about every dish but is just as delicious on its own with hot steamed rice. I love it as an accompaniment to plain rice or roti and a dry meat dish such as lamb chops, cutlets or tandoori chicken. Tarka refers to the final step where the mix of spices is fried in oil or ghee until sizzling and aromatic. My kids really enjoyed this as toothless toddlers whilst I was weaning them onto life in the curry lane. Being cheap, delicious and healthy, tarka dhal is the perfect comfort food supper (especially for the skint student foodie!).

Serves 4-6

250 grams of red lentils
1/2 teaspoon of turmeric
1.2 litres of water
Salt
1/2 teaspoon of chilli powder
225 grams of canned tomatoes or 4 fresh tomatoes, skinned and diced
1 tablespoon of lemon juice
4 tablespoons of oil or ghee
1 small onion, finely chopped
1/2 teaspoon of mustard seeds
1 teaspoon of cumin seeds
2 cloves of garlic, sliced into thin strands or slices

Place the lentils, turmeric, water and salt in a large pan and bring to boil. Skim off any scum and simmer over a medium heat for 20 minutes.

Stir in the chilli, tomatoes and lemon juice and cook for a further 10 minutes. Depending upon how you prefer your dhal to look, you may wish to leave the mixture so you can see the individual lentils or, using a hand blender, blend the mixture to a smooth consistency.

Meanwhile, in a heavy based frying pan, fry the sliced onion in 1 tablespoon of the oil or ghee until it is slightly darker than golden brown. Remove the onion with a slotted spoon and set aside.

In the same pan fry the mustard seeds, cumin seeds and the garlic slices until the seeds start crackling and the garlic slices turn golden brown. This is known as the tarka.

Immediately add this mixture to the dhal and then cover the pan with a lid in order to retain the aroma and flavours of the tarka.

Before serving garnish with the fried onion.

Hyderabadi Khuti Dhal

This dish has its origins from the Mughal era of the Qutub Shahs that ruled Hyderabad. Being a "pukki" (traditional) Indian Hyderabadi, the aroma of this dhal always takes me back to my childhood holidays where I would be sat perched on my grandfather's lap whilst enjoying a polo match on the green. Over there it was a way of life and we were very privileged to have experienced it. On these days, khutti dhal was always one of the usual suspects on the menu. This is a lentil soup with a slight tangy flavour due to the tamarind and then finished off with a mix of spices sizzling in hot oil which is then poured on top of the dhal. If you can't get hold of tamarind, then use the juice of lemons or limes in equal amount to the tamarind pulp.

Serves 6

300 grams red lentils, washed
2 tomatoes, chopped
15 - 20 curry leaves
1/2 teaspoon ginger paste (refer to glossary)
1/2 teaspoon garlic paste (refer to glossary)
1/2 teaspoon chilli powder
1/4 teaspoon turmeric
1 teaspoon ground coriander
4 green chillies, cut into small pieces
5 tablespoons whole coriander leaves
5 tablespoons tamarind pulp (refer to glossary) or 2 teaspoons of tamarind paste.
Salt to taste

For Bhaghar:
1/2 teaspoon cumin seeds
3 - 4 red chillies, whole
8 - 10 whole garlic cloves, peeled
10 - 15 curry leaves
5 - 6 tablespoons ghee or vegetable oil

Put the washed lentils in a heavy based pan with the tomatoes, curry leaves, ginger and garlic.

Add 5 - 6 cups of water and bring to boil. When the lentils are tender, drain out the water.

To the boiled lentils, add the turmeric, chilli powder, ground coriander and salt. Then add the tamarind and cook on a medium heat for 5 - 10 minutes.

Add the coriander and green chillies.

For the bhaghar, heat the ghee or oil and then add the garlic cloves, red chillies, cumin seeds and curry leaves. When the red chillies become a dark colour, pour the whole mixture over the dhal and cover immediately.

Breads & Rice

If I had a penny for every time I have been asked how to cook rice, I would be writing this book from my private yacht! Even though I tell everyone how simple it is, I can recall a heated debate I had with my husband at university before we were married on this very subject, which resulted in my ringing a friend to clarify which of us was right. Neither of us was, and in order to avoid any future confrontation my very trusted friend bought a rice cooker for our wedding present.

I will explain in this book how to make perfect fluffy rice. In fact, I will show you how to make a range of popular rice dishes and once you get the knack you will find it surprisingly easy. As rice is a staple, Indian cooks have invented a wide range of interesting ways to prepare it, both separately, such as a classic pilau rice, or as an integral part of the dish, as in chicken or lamb biryani.

Bread is to the north of India what rice is to the south. Most supermarkets nowadays stock a range of plain and filled Indian breads but there is nothing like the taste and smell of fresh homemade rotis and naans. They are both fun and satisfying to make at home. Don't worry, with a bit of practice and after lots of very strange shaped breads, you will soon get the hang of it.

Naan Bread

If there is anything that will make you fall in love with Indian food, it will be fresh naans. This is the authentic recipe for homemade naans and once you have tried this and realised how simple they are to make, you will never ever be tempted to buy the stodgy supermarket versions again. The aroma of the naans as they are cooking will fill your house and your heart. Naan is so versatile – put lashings of butter on top to make butter naan, garlic pieces and butter on top to make garlic naan…the list goes on. I always add fresh coriander and either whole cumin seeds or carom (ajwain) seeds to the dough. The taste is so amazing with just about any kind of curry. This recipe will make you the best naans you have ever tasted outside of a good Indian restaurant. Definitely one with which to impress friends and family at the next dinner party.

Makes 8

2 tablespoons of fresh yeast or 1 sachet (5 grams) of dried yeast
120 ml of warm milk
2 tablespoons of sugar
120 ml of natural yoghurt
1 large egg, lightly beaten
3 tablespoons of oil plus extra for brushing
Salt to taste
450 grams of plain flour plus extra for brushing
3 tablespoons of warm water (optional)
1 tablespoon of black onion seeds

Dissolve the yeast in 3 tablespoons of the warm milk.

Stir in 1 teaspoon of sugar and leave to rest in a warm place for 10 minutes until fluffy.

Lightly beat the yoghurt and add the remaining sugar and milk, the egg, the 3 tablespoons of oil and salt to taste.

Stir in the yeast mixture and flour and mix to a dough.

Knead for 10 to 15 minutes until smooth, using extra water if necessary and dusting with flour to prevent sticking.

Cover the dough with a damp cloth and set aside for 4 hours until doubled in size.

Punch down the dough and knead it for 2 minutes until smooth.

Divide it into 8 equal balls and roll out to 20 cm circles.

Brush with a little oil and sprinkle with onion seeds.

Place 2 breads on a greased baking sheet and bake in a pre-heated oven at 240 degrees C, gas mark 9, for 3 minutes until the bread is puffed up and has turned golden brown.

When the naans are ready keep them warm in a clean, dry kitchen towel.

Tip:
You can be very versatile when making naans. I often add chopped fresh coriander and cumin seeds instead of the black onion seeds. They also tastes very nice with carom (ajwain) seeds. During the baking you can brush the naans with melted butter. I often use garlic butter.

Kheema Naan

Stuffed naans are always a delight to eat, but eating kheema naan takes you to another dimension. Whenever I have had this in a typical Indian restaurant on the high street I have always found that the naan has been of good standard only to be completely let down by the minced, bright red tandoori meat in the middle. The kheema, or lamb mince, has to be of good quality and lean or the naan will end up being saturated in the fat of the mince. The best kheema naan I ever ate was in Lahore in Pakistan. It was the highlight of my great eat-out adventure there.

Makes 12

1 quantity of naan dough (refer to the recipe for naan bread)
1 tablespoon of oil
1 small onion, finely chopped
350 grams of lean lamb, minced
1 teaspoon of ground coriander
1 teaspoon of ground roasted cumin
1/2 teaspoon of garam masala (refer to Glossary)
1/2 teaspoon of ground red chilli
Salt to taste
6 1/2 tablespoons of water
2 tablespoons of chopped fresh coriander
1 small green chilli, chopped

Prepare the dough as for naan bread and set aside for 1 hour.

Heat the oil and fry the onion until golden brown.

Stir in the meat, ground coriander, cumin and red chilli, salt and the water. Bring to the boil and then cover and simmer gently for 15 minutes until the meat is tender.

Remove the lid and draw off any remaining liquid over a high heat.

Leave to cool.

Mix in the coriander, green chilli and garam masala.

Punch down the dough and knead it for 2 minutes until smooth.

Divide into 12 equal balls and roll out 20 cm circles.

Divide the filling mixture into 12 portions and place one in the centre of each round of dough. Seal the edges together over the filling and roll out very gently in order to flatten slightly but being careful not to tear the surface of the dough and expose the meat.

Place 2 breads on a greased baking sheet and bake in a pre-heated oven at 240 degrees C, gas mark 9, for 3 minutes until the bread is puffed up and has turned golden brown. Whilst it is cooking brush with melted butter.

Chapatis

Makes 12

350 grams of ata flour or whole
   meal flour, plus extra for dusting
1 level teaspoon of salt
250 ml of warm milk, water or
   buttermilk
1 tablespoon of oil

This is an Indian light flatbread and the perfect accompaniment to most Indian dishes. This needs to be cooked on a flat skillet over a high heat. The dough is unleavened. The secret is to make the chapatis round and thin and if they manage to puff up when cooking then give yourself a pat on the back because it means you have mastered the art of making chapatis.

Mix together the flour, salt and milk, water or buttermilk to form a dough.

Place the dough on a floured surface and knead in the oil.

Knead for about 10 minutes until smooth then cover with a damp cloth and leave to stand at room temperature for about 10 to 20 minutes.

Divide the dough into 12 balls. Coat each one with flour and flatten to form a round.

Roll out to about 15 cm in diameter.

Heat an iron griddle, tava or a frying pan over a high heat then reduce the heat to medium.

Place one chapati in the hot pan and cook for about 30 seconds until the top begins to puff up.

Turn over the chapati and cook for a further 30 to 40 seconds until the surface starts to puff up.

Remove from the pan and cook the remaining chapatis in the same way. Keep the cooked chapatis warm in a clean kitchen towel while you cook the remaining ones.

Paratha

Makes 12

225 grams of whole meal flour,
  plus extra for dusting
100 grams of plain white flour
1 level teaspoon of salt
250 ml of warm water, milk or
  buttermilk
120 ml of vegetable oil

This literally translates into "layers of cooked dough". A paratha without the layers is not a paratha, it is just a roti dabbed in oil. There is nothing like a flaky, crispy paratha to go with your favourite Indian dish. This is lovely, multi-layered, rustically crisp on the outside pastry-like bread. I warn you, it's heavy but a real treat to have once in a while. To make this, ensure that you have a flat wide frying pan or a "tava", which is the traditional skillet and can be purchased from most Asian stores.

Mix the flours and salt. Work in the water, milk or buttermilk and 1 tablespoon of oil to make a dough.

Knead for 10 minutes and then cover with a damp cloth and leave to rest for 20 minutes.

Divide the dough into 12 equal balls and taking one at a time, roll each out into a circle. Brush each circle with a little oil, fold in half then brush with oil and fold again to make a triangle. Dust with flour and flatten with a rolling pin to make either a circle or a triangle making sure they are about half a centimentre in thickness.

Heat a frying pan over a medium heat. Traditionally a tava is used. This is a special cast iron skillet specially made for cooking rotis and can be purchased from any Asian store. Please don't worry if you don't have a tava as a normal wide base frying pan will do.

Once you have rolled out the dough place it very carefully on the hot tava or frying pan and leave for about 2 minutes. Regularly check the base of the dough and turn over when brown blotches appear on the face of the paratha.

Cook in exactly the same way on the other side of the paratha and flip it over when the brown blotches appear.

At this point brush the paratha with vegetable oil and turn immediately repeating the same process on the other side.

Continue to cook on both side until it starts to puff up.

Remove from the pan and keep warm while you fry the remaining parathas.

Plain Boiled/Steamed Rice

This is a straightforward easy guide to getting perfect rice. I have used this method hundreds of times whether cooking for a catering order of 100 or just one person. It works superbly and will produce fluffy and tasty rice every time. It is one of the few recipes in this book that requires precision timing. When cooking any kind of rice, whether it be plain, pilau or biryani, always concentrate on the dish and nothing else otherwise the rice may become overcooked and stodgy.

Serves 4–6

250 grams, or 1 cup, of basmati rice
500 ml or 2 cups of water
1 tablespoon of ghee or vegetable oil.
Salt to taste

Always use the same size cup to measure the rice and the water. It is important to use one cup of rice to two cups of water when making plain boiled rice. Place the rice, water and ghee in a pan and bring to the boil over a medium heat.

Reduce the heat to low, cover the pan with a lid that fits securely and cook for a further 15 to 20 minutes, at a simmer. At no time should you lift the lid during cooking to check on the rice or stir it.

Turn off the heat and leave for at least 5 minutes before serving.

Separate the grains with a fork and serve hot.

Aromatic Rice (Pilau Rice)

This is a process whereby rice is cooked in a seasoned broth. This is a perfect base to any Indian curry. Remember that cooking rice correctly is a culinary trick worth learning. All you need to do is give it a little thought and minimal interference.

Serves 4

250 grams. or 1 cup of basmati rice. soaked
250 ml. or 1 cup. of water
3 tablespoons of ghee
1 onion. sliced
1 cm of cinnamon stick
3 cardamom pods
3 cloves
1/2 teaspoon of cumin seeds
Salt to taste

Heat the ghee in a heavy based saucepan and fry the onions until browned.

Add the cinnamon, cardamom pods, cloves and cumin seeds and fry for 1 minute.

Add the rice and fry for 2 to 3 minutes, stirring constantly.

Add the water and salt and bring to the boil. Cover and simmer gently for 15 minutes until the rice is cooked.

Kashmiri-Style Chicken Pilau

This is wonderfully fragrant and has become a popular and much loved dish. I got this recipe from a trusted Kashmiri friend whose family through the generations has maintained this traditional recipe. This dish is just bursting with rich flavours and whole spices. The nuts and the raisins add crunchiness and sweetness to the dish. This is a perfect choice for those people who find it hard to eat hot Indian cuisine. It goes really well with a lovely vegetarian dish such as potato and cauliflower curry. Alternatively, if you want to add more meat to the feast, go for boti kebab or just tandoori chicken. Personally, I just prefer to eat it with a dollop of yoghurt on the side as it's a meal in itself.

Serves 6

1.5 kilograms of whole chicken, cut into portions (reserving the wings, neck and giblets)
3 litres, or 12 cups, of water
25 grams of pistachios
2 teaspoons of fennel seeds
2 tablespoons of cumin seeds
1 teaspoon of paprika
1 tablespoon of garam masala (refer to Glossary)
3 tablespoons of natural yoghurt
1 teaspoon of saffron strands
3 tablespoons of hot milk
5 tablespoons of vegetable oil
2 onions, chopped
25 grams of blanched almonds
50 grams of raisins
3 cardamom pods
2 cinnamon sticks
1/2 teaspoon of cloves
2 bay leaves
1/2 teaspoon of black peppercorns
1/4 teaspoon of grated nutmeg
5 cloves of garlic, chopped
Salt to taste
2 tablespoon of chopped fresh mint
675 grams, or 3 cups, of long grain rice, soaked

Boil the chicken wings, neck and giblets in 250 ml of the water to make 250 ml of stock.

Grind the pistachios, fennel seeds, cumin seeds, paprika and garam masala and then whisk them into the yoghurt.

Soak the saffron in hot milk for 15 minutes.

Heat 4 tablespoons of oil and fry the onions until browned. Then remove the onions with a slotted spoon and set aside.

Fry the almonds and raisins until golden.

Add the cardamom, cinnamon, cloves, bay leaves, peppercorns, nutmeg and garlic and fry for 1 to 2 minutes.

Mix in the ground spices from Step 2 and cook for 1 to 2 minutes, stirring occasionally.

Add the chicken, salt and strained stock. Cover and simmer for 15 minutes, stirring occasionally, until the chicken is half cooked and the gravy is thick.

Stir in the mint.

Boil the rice in the remaining water and oil for 8 minutes until almost cooked, then drain.

Transfer the chicken to a casserole dish and cover it with the rice. Then garnish with the almonds, the fried onions and raisins and pour over the saffron milk.

Cover tightly with foil and put the lid on top. Bake in a pre-heated oven at 200 degrees C, gas mark 6, for 15 minutes.

Reduce the oven temperature to 150 degrees C, gas mark 2, and cook for a further 15 minutes.

Rice with Chickpeas

This is a lovely variation on plain steamed rice with the added satisfaction of the chickpeas for nutrition. I often pack this in my Tupperware to take to work for lunch and have it hot with a dollop of plain yoghurt. Five minutes later, there is usually a crowd of salivating colleagues around me often having the cheek to ask why I didn't bring any in for them.

Serves 6

75 grams of chickpeas, soaked overnight. Alternatively a 250 grams can of ready cooked chickpeas, drained
2.5 cm of cinnamon stick
4 cardamom pods
8 cloves of garlic
1/2 teaspoon of chilli powder
1 green chilli
1/2 teaspoon of ground turmeric
1 teaspoon of mango powder
500 grams, or 2 cups, of basmati rice, soaked
3 tablespoons of vegetable oil
6 spring onions, chopped
1 teaspoon of grated ginger
1 teaspoon of cumin seeds
4 bay leaves
1 teaspoon of black pepper
Salt to taste

Drain the liquid from the chickpeas. Place the chickpeas, cinnamon, cardamoms, garlic, chilli powder, green chilli, turmeric and mango powder in a pan and just cover with water. Bring to the boil then cover and simmer for about 2 hours if you are using dried chickpeas until the peas are tender. If you are using the ready cooked chickpeas follow the same process but simmer for 30 minutes instead of 2 hours.

Drain, reserving the liquid, and discard the herbs. Make the liquid up to 1 litre with water.

Heat the oil and fry the onions until golden.

Add the ginger and fry for 2 minutes.

Add the cumin seeds, bay leaves, pepper and chickpeas and fry for 3 to 4 minutes, stirring occasionally.

Add the rice and fry for 2 minutes, stirring occasionally.

Add the liquid you have previously reserved from the chickpeas and bring to the boil. Then cover and simmer gently for about 30 minutes until the water has been absorbed.

Separate the grains with a fork and serve hot.

Classic Hyderabadi Biryani

When I asked my mother for this recipe, she gave it to me willingly. When I told her it was going to be included in my book, she looked at me sheepishly. I can say with all confidence that our "khandaan" (direct and extended family members) do make the best Hyderabadi biryani. My mother has always told me many guarded family recipe secrets and certainly this was one of them. Don't worry, she understands my necessity to share the best and most well known biryani in the world, with the world. In exchange for this act of Judas I want to say that I owe all my cooking talents to my darling mother. Essentially, this dish is made with basmati rice and lamb, although you can substitute this with chicken. The blending of Mughlai and Andra Pradesh cuisines in the kitchen of the Nizam, ruler of the historic Hyderabad state, resulted in the creation of Hyderabadi biryani. This dish is so close to my heart as it evokes vivid memories of my very early childhood when we would visit family in Hyderabad, and particularly when we would have days out to the farmhouses on "shikkar". This is when the men went hunting whilst the women would prepare a feast to meet these brave huntsmen upon their return. I recall my crestfallen brother coming back from a day of shikkar having only caught a rabbit! Everyone's eyes would light up at the appearance of the fresh biryani made on a traditional stove. This is one of those dishes that I only perfected after trying it a few times. I can only describe it as manna from heaven.

Serves 6

500 grams of lamb. Mixture of shoulder and leg with bone in and cut into bite sized portions
500 grams of basmati rice
1 teaspoon of garam masala (refer to Glossary)
250 ml or 1 cup of water for the meat
6 whole cardamoms
1.5 litres or 6 cups of water for the rice
3 cinnamon sticks (2.5 cm long)
5 cloves
3 bay leaves
1/4 teaspoon black zeera (black cumin seeds – refer to Glossary)
1/4 cup of lemon juice

3 tablespoons of vegetable oil
100 grams of butter
1/2 teaspoon of saffron threads soaked in 2 tablespoons of hot milk
3 medium onions, finely sliced and fried until golden brown
1 tablespoon of ginger puree (refer to Glossary)
1 tablespoon of garlic puree (refer to Glossary)
1 teaspoon of red chilli powder
1 teaspoon of turmeric
Salt to taste
6 tablespoons of chopped fresh coriander
5 to 6 green chillies, cut into pieces
8 to 10 fresh mint leaves
125 ml or 1/2 cup of fresh single cream
125 grams of natural yoghurt

Continued on next page.

Classic Hyderabadi Biryani cont.

Marinate the lamb in the yoghurt, garam masala, 4 tablespoons of fresh coriander, 7 mint leaves, ginger puree, garlic puree, salt, turmeric and red chilli powder for 2 hours in the refrigerator.

In a heavy based pan heat the 3 tablespoons of vegetable oil and add 3⁄4 of the fried onions and the marinated meat. Stir on a high heat until the meat is sealed. Then lower the temperature and add one cup or 250 ml of water. Cover and cook, stirring occasionally, until the meat is tender and the water has reduced to half its amount.

In a separate broad, heavy based pan, boil the 6 cups or 1.5 litres of water. Then add salt (about 1⁄2 a teaspoon), cardamoms, black zeera, cinnamon, cloves, chillies and bay leaves. Add the rice and continue to boil, stirring occasionally, until the rice is half cooked. This can be tested by taking a grain and seeing whether it splits in half easily. At this stage, strain the rice and keep aside in a sieve.

Into the same broad pan as in Step 3, which is now empty, put a few slices of the butter and then spread on top half the rice. On top of this put half the saffron and milk mixture, half the lemon juice, some of the remaining fried onions and coriander. On top of this spread all the cooked lamb with the juices. Then spread on top of this layer the rest of the rice and ensure the meat is fully covered. Finally, sprinkle on top of the rice the remaining saffron milk, lemon juice, fresh coriander, fried onions, butter in pieces, cream and remaining mint leaves.

Ensure the lid of the pan is then secured tightly so that no steam can escape, and cook on a low flame for about 25 to 30 minutes, at which point the rice will be fully cooked. Carefully mix the layers in the pan just before serving.

Cold Side Dishes

These usually consist of salads, chutneys, pickles and dips. No Indian table is complete without a mass of little dishes containing sauces, chutneys and pickles – all providing extra flavour or piquancy. In some ways, these are just as important as the main dishes.

I love a variety of condiments to perk up my Indian meal. It balances the meal whilst at the same time teases the palate with sharp contrasts of sweet, sour, hot and salty flavours. These can be anything from simple cucumber wedges seasoned with salt, pepper, cayenne pepper and lemon juice to carefully prepared pickles that can be kept for a year.

Yoghurt (raita) is a firm favourite as a side dish with any Indian meal. It provides that much-needed cooking contrast. I often keep a selection of raitas in my fridge with carrot or cucumber sticks handy to ward off the incoming traffic of those complaining of being tired, hot and hungry. It is a great alternative to the crisp cupboard!

Tomato Kachumbar

This is essentially a spicy tomato, cucumber and onion relish. In Hindi, it literally means tiny pieces of raw vegetables. Allow the dish to rest before serving so all the flavours can blend in. It's an Indian version of a Mexican salsa. It's ridiculously simple and adds a great accompaniment to your entrees, be it rice, pilaus or rotis. Personally, I love it with grilled meat and fresh naan.

Serves 6

125 ml of lime juice
1/2 teaspoon of sugar
Salt to taste
6 tomatoes, chopped
1/2 a cucumber, chopped
8 spring onions, chopped
1 fresh green chilli, de-seeded and
    chopped
1 tablespoon of chopped fresh
    coriander
1 tablespoon of chopped fresh mint

Mix the lime juice, sugar and a pinch of salt together in a large bowl and stir until the sugar has completely dissolved.

Add the tomatoes, cucumber, spring onions, chilli, coriander and mint and toss well to mix. Chop all the vegetables into fairly small, even sized pieces for the best texture and presentation. You can generally use any vegetables you have in the refrigerator, as long as they can be eaten raw.

Cover with cling film and leave to chill in the refrigerator for at least 30 minutes. Toss the vegetables before serving.

Spicy Potato Salad

Serves 4

This is a great pot-luck or picnic dish. It always gets gobbled up quickly no matter how much of it I prepare so I always keep a sneaky stash of it in the fridge hidden from view, just for myself. This goes just as well with western food as it does with Indian food. It's a great way to pep up your regular potato salad with a twist.

450 grams of potatoes, halved if large, left unpeeled
Salt and pepper to taste
4 tablespoons of ghee or vegetable oil
1 teaspoon of cumin seeds
225 ml of natural yoghurt
1/2 teaspoon of chilli powder
1 tablespoon of chopped fresh coriander

Cook the potatoes in a large saucepan of lightly salted boiling water for 20 minutes, or until tender.

Drain and leave until cool enough to handle. Peel the cooled potatoes, if you like, and cut into small dice. When you dice the potatoes, try to make sure that all the pieces are the same size so they cook evenly.

Heat the ghee in a large, heavy based frying pan and add half the cumin seeds and all the potatoes. Keep tossing the potatoes over the heat to brown on all sides. Cook over a low heat for 10 minutes, stirring constantly until all the potatoes are golden brown all over. Remove with a slotted spoon and leave to cool completely.

Mix together in a bowl the yoghurt, chilli powder, coriander, the remaining cumin seeds and salt and pepper to taste.

Add the potatoes and toss well to mix. Taste and adjust the seasoning and chill before serving.

Coconut Raita

This is a South Indian raita recipe. "Raita" is essentially a condiment made with yoghurt and used as a sauce or a dip. The yoghurt is usually seasoned. I learnt this one from a South Indian friend and, boy, does it refresh the palette. This fragrant raita works well as a starter with some poppadoms or naan bread as well as a cool friend to accompany a nice spicy fish curry.

Serves 4

3 tablespoons of grated coconut
4 green chillies
1 teaspoon of chopped ginger
4 tablespoons of chopped fresh
    coriander
250 ml of natural yoghurt
Salt to taste
2 teaspoons of vegetable oil
1 teaspoon of mustard seeds
1 teaspoon of yellow split peas
1/2 teaspoon of split black beans
1/4 teaspoon of cumin seeds
1 dried red chilli, halved
1/4 teaspoon asafoetida
2 curry leaves

Boil the yellow split peas and black beans separately until tender. Drain and keep aside.

Grind the coconut, chillies, ginger and a little of the coriander to a paste.

Add the yoghurt with salt to taste and mix well.

Heat the oil and fry the remaining ingredients until the mustard seeds start crackling and the split peas are golden.

Add to the yoghurt mixture and serve garnished with the remaining coriander.

Spicy Cucumber Raita

This is a really soothing and cooling yoghurt dish to have, especially for the times when you're struggling with the heat of your curry. It's also perfect for dipping crusty triangles of pitta bread in as a starter.

Serves 4–6

1 cucumber
600 ml of natural yoghurt
Pepper
2 green chillies, chopped
2 tablespoons of chopped fresh
    coriander
1 teaspoon of cumin seeds
1/2 teaspoon of garam masala
    (refer to Glossary)

Peel the cucumber and grate it coarsely.

Squeeze out the excess moisture.

Beat the yoghurt then stir in the cucumber and pepper and spoon into a serving bowl.

Sprinkle with the chillies and coriander.

Dry roast the cumin seeds for a few seconds until golden then grind and sprinkle over the yoghurt.

Dry roast the garam masala for a few seconds until darkened then sprinkle over the raita and serve.

Mint and Aubergine Raita

This is an easy side dish for a cheerful barbecue evening that compliments just about anything. You, like me, will find yourself making this very often. This particular raita is very aromatic because of the herbs and spices and it tastes superbly fresh and nutty. This is a snack you can keep in the fridge and happily eat on a daily basis without feeling guilty.

Serves 4

1 aubergine, cut into 2.5 cm pieces
450 ml of natural yoghurt
Pinch of ground red chilli
1/2 teaspoon of ground roasted
    cumin
Salt to taste
1 tablespoon of chopped fresh mint
1 small onion, thinly sliced
1 spring onion, thinly sliced

Steam the aubergine for 10 minutes then mash it with a fork and set aside to cool.

Mix together the remaining ingredients.

Stir in the mashed aubergine and chill before serving.

Aubergine Pickle

Makes 1.5 kilograms,
or 4 lbs

This is a deliciously unique pickle that's made up of a blend of aubergine and spices. You may be tempted to buy this one readymade off the shelf, but please resist; it's not that difficult to make at home. This one got a real thumbs-up at home. I love to eat this at night with cheese and bread. It reminds me a bit of an Indian version of Branston Pickle.

175 litres of wine vinegar
10 grams of dried red chillies
1 tablespoon of ground turmeric
25 grams of ginger, sliced
12 cloves of garlic, sliced
300 ml of gingelly oil
1 teaspoon of fenugreek seeds
1 teaspoon of cumin seeds
1 teaspoon of mustard seeds
2 sprigs of fresh curry leaves
1.5 kilograms of small aubergines, quartered
8 green chillies
1 teaspoon of sugar
Salt to taste

Grind the red chillies, turmeric, half the ginger and half the garlic in 150 ml of the wine vinegar.

Heat the oil and fry the fenugreek, cumin and mustard seeds, curry leaves and remaining garlic and ginger until brown.

Add the ground paste and continue to fry until dry.

Add the aubergines and green chillies and pour in enough of the remaining wine vinegar to cover the vegetables.

Add the sugar and salt and simmer until the aubergines are tender and the oil floats to the top.

Leave to cool and then put into airtight jars.

Cauliflower Pickle

This makes about 900
grams

This is so addictive! It goes very well with just about any meal, even in sandwiches. Indian pickles are almost too good to be called condiments. No matter how much you eat these pickles and with what, they are intended to enhance a dish and add new dimensions to flavour.

900 grams of cauliflower, cut into florets
Salt to taste
1 tablespoon of mustard seeds
50 grams of mango powder
1 tablespoon of chilli powder
2 teaspoons of ground turmeric
1 teaspoon of aniseeds
6 tablespoons of mustard oil

Cook the cauliflower in boiling salted water until just tender but not too soft.

Drain and leave to cool.

Grind together the remaining ingredients to make a paste.

Toss the cooked cauliflower in the paste and leave to marinate for one day in a warm place. Then put into airtight jars and store in a cool place.

South Indian Lime Pickle

The humble lime is so versatile and lends itself beautifully to pickling. This is one spicy, tangy pickle that you can eat with pretty much anything. Make this at home and stop relying on the readymade, jarred versions in shops with their preservative cloned aftertaste. Until you have tried making it, leave it to your imagination how good this pickle really is.

Makes 150 grams

150 ml of water
100 grams of jaggery
2 teaspoons of salt
1/2 teaspoon of coriander seeds
1/2 teaspoon of garam masala
   (refer to Glossary)
1 teaspoon of fennel seeds
1/2 teaspoon of Nigella seeds
15 limes, quartered

Put all the ingredients except the limes into a pan and cook over a medium heat for 10 minutes.

Place the lime quarters in a glass jar and spoon in the cooked mixture.

Shake the jar thoroughly and leave in a warm place for about one week until the lime skin is tender, shaking at least once a day.

Transfer the mixture into an airtight container and store in a cool place. Shake the limes before each use.

Tamarind Chutney

This has been my favourite chutney ever since I was a kid. It's sweet and sour whilst being quite mellow and so easy to make. It's easily the most exciting condiment in the Indian repertoire and perfect for dipping your favourite snacks in. I searched high and low for the perfect tamarind chutney recipe for years and I believe now I have found it. The sweet, tart taste of tamarind is unmistakable and definitely delicious. Interestingly enough, tamarind is internationally known for its medicinal properties as well. What I can say is that it's definitely taken the place of tomato sauce on our dinner table.

Makes 675 grams

100 grams of dried tamarind
300 ml of water
225 grams of sugar
1 teaspoon of garam masala (refer
   to Glossary)
1 teaspoon of ground roasted
   cumin
12 teaspoon of ground red chilli
Salt to taste
75 grams of raisins
5 dried dates, thinly sliced

Soak the tamarind overnight in the water or boil it for 15 minutes over a medium to low heat.

Sieve the pulp and discard the seeds and stalks (the waste should not exceed 1 tablespoon).

Place the pulp, sugar and spices in a pan over a high heat and bring to boil, then simmer gently for 10 minutes.

Add the raisins and dates and cook for a further 2 to 3 minutes.

Leave to cool and then spoon into airtight jars and leave in a cool place.

Hot Garlic Pickle

Pickles are just an integral part of the Indian meal. You know it's a good one when your mouth starts watering just writing about it. The aroma of garlic is unmistakable and pungent so oil your hands before you peel garlic to prevent your fingers from getting discoloured and having a lingering garlic aroma throughout the day. Soaking the garlic cloves in hot water makes it easier to peel them. Garlic is an excellent source of dietary manganese. This pickle will keep in your fridge for about three months, but I guarantee it won't last that long.

Makes 1.75 kilograms

175 kilograms of garlic
225 grams of salt
2 teaspoons of ground turmeric
1 teaspoon of mustard seeds
1 teaspoon of fenugreek seeds
1 teaspoon of aniseeds
1 teaspoon of Nigella seeds
1 teaspoon of cumin seeds
225 grams of mango powder
100 grams of chilli powder
Mustard oil

Soak the garlic in hot water for about 15 minutes and then rub off the skins.

Dry thoroughly, and then pound lightly to mash, but not pulp. Leave a few in their whole form.

Mix the garlic with the salt and turmeric and leave to marinate in a warm place for 1 day.

Roast all the seeds lightly in a heavy based pan and then grind coarsely.

Add the garlic with the mango and chilli powders and then spoon the mixture into a large jar.

Add just enough oil to cover all the ingredients.

Cover with muslin and leave for 6 days in a warm place then transfer to small airtight jars and store in a cool place.

Mango Pickle

Makes 1.75 kilograms

6 medium mangos, semi-ripe,
  peeled, de-seeded and chopped
  into cubes
115 grams of salt
70 grams of chilli powder
25 grams of mustard powder
25 grams of ground fenugreek
1 tablespoon of turmeric
300 ml of mustard oil
15 grams of yellow mustard seeds
  (crushed)
1/2 teaspoon of asafoetida

This Indian-style pickle is divine and combines the sweetness of mango with the tart of the spice, giving that warm, rich Indian touch. It's a great savoury condiment and it's my favourite holiday gift to friends. Prepare it a couple of weeks in advance as it won't taste as good if eaten immediately after making.

Pack the mango pieces into a jar that is large, sterilised and preferably heat resistant.

Sprinkle over the salt.

Cover and leave to stand in a warm place for 10–14 days or until the mangos have turned brown and softened.

Mix the chilli powder, mustard powder, fenugreek and turmeric together in a bowl and add to the jar of mangos.

Stir the mix, then re-cover and leave to stand for 2 days.

If your jar is not heatproof, transfer the whole mixture into a heatproof bowl.

Heat the mustard seeds and asafoetida in the oil and cook, stirring constantly, until the oil is very hot and just beginning to smoke.

Pour the oil and spices over the mangos and mix well, then cover and leave to cool.

If not already in the jar, transfer the mixture to the sterilised jar now, seal and store in a sunny place for about a week before eating it.

Sweet Dishes

Those with a sweet tooth can really indulge in the sweet section of this book. The traditional Indian sweets such as gulab jamun, ladu, barfi and jalebi are delicious but I have always found them a guilty pleasure and they have always left me wondering, first, how much damage they are doing to my pearly whites and, second, how many days I would have to suffer in the gym to burn off just a mouthful. The amount of sugar you add is simply a guide; you are free to add or subtract to taste. On occasions, I have also substituted the sugar with a good sweetener. I find a small portion is a delicious pleaser after the lingering spiciness of the main meal's dishes.

Due to the richness of the sweets, always use a non-stick saucepan if possible because some of them stick to the pan very easily during cooking.

Sweets play an important role in India. No function festival is celebrated without sweets. Sweets are always distributed amongst relatives, friends and neighbours whenever a child is born, a marriage takes place, or at birthdays or other celebrations. It is a lovely way to encourage celebration and bring people closer together.

Kheer (Indian Rice Pudding)

This is an Indian rice pudding with a twist. An Indian festival without kheer is like Halloween without pumpkins. Unlike most of the Indian sweets, this one is very simple and easy to make and, in fact, bringing out the richness whilst using very simple ingredients is what makes it "numero uno" in my opinion. It's totally worth it if you haven't made it before and a real family favourite. My mother is a die hard fan of this sweet.

Serves 4

1.75 litres of full cream milk
2 tablespoons of basmati rice
4 tablespoons of sugar
1 1/2 tablespoons of sultanas
3 tablespoons of finely chopped
   blanched almonds
1/2 pistachios. chopped
1/2 teaspoon of ground cardamom
1/4 teaspoon of ground saffron
1 teaspoon of rose water (kewra)

Bring the milk to the boil then reduce the heat to medium to low.

Add the rice and simmer for 1 hour, stirring occasionally.

Mix in half the nuts, the cardamom, the sugar, sultanas and the saffron and simmer gently for 45 minutes or until the rice is at the desired consistency.

Remove from the heat and mix in the rose water.

Sprinkle with the remaining nuts before serving. This dish is usually served chilled or at room temperature.

Carrot Halwa

This is also known as gajjar ka halwa. The only really hard thing in making halwa is messing it up. It is a really versatile dessert in the sense that essences of different flavours can be added to give it a special twist, so it can be like eating a different sweet every time. This is undoubtedly my favourite type of halwa and one that gets served on my dinner table at every party due to comments like "Well, I'm definitely coming if you're making gajjar ka halwa". It's always an unavoidable part of my menu and tastes wonderful hot with lashings of whipped cream or vanilla ice cream melting on top like lava from a volcano. If I had a last request, this would be it.

Serves 8

900 grams of carrots, grated
600 ml of full fat milk
200 grams of sugar
4 tablespoons of ghee
50 grams of blanched almonds, halved
50 grams of sultanas
25 grams of pistachios, halved
150 grams of khoya (refer to Glossary)
1 teaspoon of ground cardamom

Place the carrot and milk in a heavy based pan and bring to the boil over a high heat.

Reduce the heat to medium and simmer until all the milk has been absorbed, stirring occasionally.

Add the sugar and continue to simmer until the liquid has been absorbed.

Pour in the ghee and cook gently for 10 minutes.

Stir in the nuts, khoya, sultanas and cardamom and simmer for 5 minutes.

Serve hot, ideally with a dollop of double cream or vanilla ice cream.

Almond Barfi

Barfi is originally from Persia, where it means "snow" since it's similar to ice in appearance and thus it's always served cold. It was introduced to India and Pakistan during the Mughal Empire in the 16th century. This is typically served cut into squares or diamonds and covered with a thin layer of edible metallic leaf called "vark". Whenever I see this dessert dressed up this way, it always reminds me of weddings. Then, the barfi is suitably dressed for the occasion, covered in vark and presented in an ornately decorated tray in a bid to outshine the bride. This is what I would describe as an Indian version of fudge. It's so versatile that whilst doing my research on barfi I came across 48 different types from beetroot to papaya barfi.

Makes 12

100 grams of ground almonds
50 grams of sugar
2 1/2 tablespoons of water
1/4 tablespoon of ground carda-
    mom
1 tablespoon crushed pistachios for
    garnish
1/4 teaspoon of safron threads for
    garnish

Boil the sugar and water together for 2 to 3 minutes until a drop in a cup of cold water sets and stays at the bottom. Then turn off the heat.

Stir in the almonds and cardamom and mix thoroughly until smooth. Then cool the mixture.

When cooled, form the mixture into a ball and place on a greased plate. Flatten into a square shape about 5 mm thick.

Cut into squares or triangles.

Sprinkle garnish ingredients of pistachio nuts and safron at the end.

Cashew Nut Barfi

This is a popular Indian sweet made of powdered cashew nut and sugar syrup. You must ensure the nuts are finely ground and that the sugar syrup is the right consistency for this recipe to work. It is the key to its success. This is such a delicious treat for any occasion and goes very well with a hot cup of tea when unexpected, but most welcome, guests pop in. Once you have cut it into squares or diamond shapes, keep it in an airtight container chilled in the fridge, where it will keep for a couple of weeks; but that's if it lasts that long. This is tongue ticklingly delicious.

Makes 20

225 grams of cashew nuts, finely
    ground
100 grams of sugar
3 1/2 tablespoons of water
1 teaspoon of rose water

Bring the water and sugar to boil then simmer until it forms a syrup. This will take around 2 to 3 minutes. Test it by putting a drop in a cup of cold water to see if it sets and stays at the bottom.

Stir in the nuts and then remove from the heat. Stir until smooth and cool.

Stir in the rose water and allow to cool further.

When completely cool shape into a round ball and spread on a greased plate so it is about 1 cm thick.

Leave this to set for 3 to 4 hours then cut into 2.5 cm squares.

Gulab Jamun

Makes 20

This dish is definitely up your street if you have a sweet tooth. It's basically a tasty Indian version of doughnuts floating in a warm sweet syrup. It gets it name from two words: "gulab" means rose and "jamun" is a kind of deep purple coloured Indian berry, probably referring to the cooked dumplings, which are dark brown in colour. Serve this warm or at room temperature by itself or hot, topped with ice cream.

100 grams of full cream milk powder
2 tablespoons of ghee, melted
2 tablespoons of plain flour
1 tablespoon of semolina
Large pinch of bicarbonate of soda (baking soda)
6 1/2 tablespoons of lukewarm milk
1/2 teaspoon of ground cardamom
Ghee and oil for deep frying
250 grams of sugar
250 ml of water

Mix together the milk powder, ghee, flour, semolina and bicarbonate of soda.

Pour in the milk and knead to a soft dough. Cover and leave for 30 minutes.

Divide into 20 equal portions and roll into balls.

Heat equal quantities of oil and ghee and fry the gulab over a medium/low heat, turning frequently. Do not fry them too quickly or they will not be cooked on the inside. Remove with a slotted spoon and leave to cool.

Meanwhile, bring the sugar, cardamom and water to boil over a medium heat and stir until the sugar has dissolved. Remove from the heat.

Add the fried gulab jamuns to the syrup. Return to the boil then simmer gently for 5 minutes.

Serve hot or cold.

Jalebis

If you have never had jalebis before, they are definitely worth a try. They are basically made by deep frying flour batter in pretzel or circular shapes, which are then soaked in sugar syrup. They are either served warm or cold and have a chewy texture with a crystallized sugary exterior coating. It is known as the national sweet of India and it's often served at festivals and celebrations. I can only describe this dish as sticky, bright golden swirls of pure pleasure that are deliciously fun to eat, particularly when piping hot served with lashings of vanilla ice cream.

Serves 6–8

450 grams of plain flour
1 teaspoon of baking powder
125 kilograms of sugar
300 ml of water
450 grams of ghee
1 teaspoon of ground saffron

Sift the flour and baking powder then add enough warm water to make a thick dough.

Boil the sugar and saffron with the water to form a thick syrup.

Heat the ghee to boiling point.

Place the dough in an icing bag and squeeze out in small spirals in the hot ghee. Fry until golden brown.

Remove from the fat and place in the syrup to soak for 5 to 10 minutes. Can be served hot or cold.

Seviyan (Vermicelli Pudding)

This dish is a real childhood memory jogger for me. I can't recall a single Eid celebration when my mother did not make Seviyan. This can only be described as a vermicelli kheer (milk pudding). You can also add cloves if you like, which gives a very subtle fragrance to the dish. It has such a rich sweet taste and can be very easily cooked with the least effort. Go ahead and enjoy it with your loved ones as much as I do with mine.

Serves 6

100 grams of fine vermicelli
1/2 teaspoon of saffron strands
500 ml of milk
50 grams of margarine
150 grams of sugar
25 grams of flaked almonds
3 tablespoons of raisins
1/2 teaspoon of ground cardamom

Break the vermicelli into 2.5 cm pieces.

Soak the saffron in 4 tablespoons of hot milk for 15 minutes.

Heat the margarine and fry the vermicelli for about 5 minutes until golden brown.

Add the remaining milk and bring to the boil, stirring constantly.

Add the saffron milk.

Cover and simmer gently for about 8 minutes until the vermicelli is tender, stirring occasionally.

Add the sugar, almonds, raisins and cardamom and stir thoroughly for 1 minute.

Serve warm or cold.

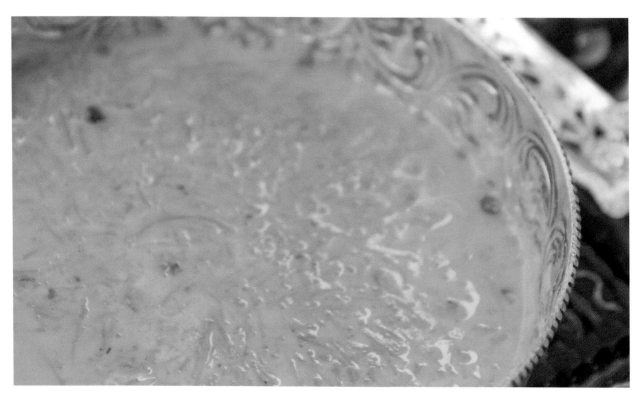

Easy Ras Malai

This is a very popular sweet dish originating in India. It literally translates into "juicy cream". It's basically made of paneer balls soaked in cream and flavoured with cardamom and, in this case, saffron as well. I don't possess a particularly sweet tooth so this dessert is ideal for me. It's easily my favourite dessert, if not Indian dish, and I love to witness the expression of surprise and contentment on people's faces when they try it for the first time. In the past I would always buy ras malai as the thought of making it (the muslin cloth technique) always exhausted me. Trust me, this method not only works but tastes better than ever. The spongy and mildly sweet paneer balls dunked in the richness of milk, creaminess of nut and mingled with flavours of cardamom and saffron – I think I just described heaven.

Serves 6

225 grams of paneer, crumbled
(refer to Glossary)
225 grams of khoya (refer to Glossary)
2 tablespoons of ghee
225 grams of sugar
15 litres of full fat milk
Pinch of ground saffron
100 grams of chopped mixed nuts
Pinch of ground cardamom
Rose water

Heat the ghee in a heavy based pan and fry the khoya for about 10 minutes over a low heat.

Add the paneer and sugar and blend thoroughly. Cook for a further 10 minutes.

Remove from the heat and divide into 12 flattened balls, shaped a bit like flying saucers.

Bring the milk to the boil. Lower the heat and simmer until reduced by half.

Remove from the heat and sprinkle with the saffron, nuts and cardamom.

Add the flying saucers then cover and leave to stand for 5 minutes.

Sprinkle with rose water before serving.

Cooking Equipment

Karahi

This is a rounded based, wok-like, non-stick pan. Its shape allows the food to move easily in the pan without sticking to the edge and thus cook evenly.

Tava

This is a shallow, concave cast-iron pan in which we cook most of our flatbreads. It's useful as the pan holds the heat well and the bread cooks quickly and evenly. Don't worry if you can't get hold of one – a non-stick frying pan will do.

Measuring Your Ingredients

This book uses metric measurements. All spoon measurements are level. A teaspoon holds 5 ml and a tablespoon holds 20 ml. The difference between one country's measuring cup and another's is, at most, within a 2 to 3 teaspoon variance. The difference is minimal and will not affect your cooking results. 1 cup holds approximately 250 ml.

Index

About the Author

Born and brought up in the UK, Shahnaaz Ayub has always been a keen cook and owes much of her inspiration to her parents, by whom she has been taught classic Hyderabadi cuisine, although she has long since widened her knowledge and passion to include the whole Indian sub-continent. Married to Shahid, whose family originate from Pakistan, Shahnaaz has also developed her skills to include classic Punjabi dishes.

Shahnaaz works as a senior trial lawyer specialising in child protection but her passion for cooking led her to start a catering company and teach classes in Indian cookery. Following the success of this, Shahnaaz was inspired to write this cookery book containing a collection of the traditional favourites. She wanted to create a "one stop shop" for Indian food.

Being a busy mother of three young children, Shahnaaz knows all too well how hectic life can be between juggling her job, her business, the family, children's activities and social life (mostly the children's as there is rarely enough time for the parents'). Despite each member of the family pursuing their own interests, what remains constant is that every evening the family sits together and enjoys a meal.

Not everyone has the time to prepare a banquet every night and that is why Shahnaaz has provided a range of delicious dishes that are easy, often quick to put together and are full of flavour.